SACRED TALES OF INDIA

D1881408

SACRED TALES OF INDIA

BY

DWIJENDRA NATH NEOGI, B. A.

WITH ILLUSTRATIONS BY

P. GHOSE

GYAN

Published by

Gyan Publishing House
5, Ansari Road
Daryaganj, New Delhi-110002
Phone: 011-47034999, 9811692060
E-mail: books@gyanbooks.com

Distribution Network
gyanbooks.com
India, USA, Canada, UK, Australia, France

© Publisher
All rights reserved. No part of this work may be reproduced, stored, adapted, or transmitted in any form or by any means, electronic, mechanical, photocopying, micro-filming, recording or otherwise, or translated in any language, without the prior written permission of the copyright owner and the publisher.

ISBN : 978-81-212-3979-0 (PB)
First Published, 1916

2nd Impression 2020

Printed at: Gyan Press, Delhi.

The book is sold subject to the condition that it shall not, by way of trade or otherwise, be lent, resold, hired out, or otherwise circulated without the prior publisher's written consent.

Sacred Tales of India
Author: Dwijendra Nath Neogi

SACRED TALES OF INDIA

BY

DWIJENDRA NATH NEOGI, B.A.

WITH ILLUSTRATIONS BY

P. GHOSE

MACMILLAN AND CO., LIMITED

ST. MARTIN'S STREET, LONDON

1916

'They changed themselves into snakes, and bidding Lahaná hold fast by their tails plunged into the water' (p. 7).

Frontispiece

BY KIND PERMISSION

MOST RESPECTFULLY DEDICATED

TO

HIS EXCELLENCY THE RIGHT HONOURABLE

THOMAS DAVID BARON CARMICHAEL OF SKIRLING,

G.C.I.E., K.C.M.G.,

OF BENGAL.

FOREWORD

About a year ago, the idea entered my mind of writing on our ceremonial lore which consists of an immense stock of curious legends transmitted from mouth to mouth for ages past. In the *zenana* of Bengal alone has the sacred fire of this knowledge been kept burning: and, were it not for our wives, sisters, and daughters, it would long since have been extinguished.

The ceremonies which I have mentioned are almost exclusively performed by women, and the sterner sex takes little or no part in them, as a rule not even knowing where or when they take place. The rites are simple and cost nothing. As to their origin, I can only hazard a guess; and it is that they have been invented at different times by Indian women of understanding above that of their contemporaries with a view to keeping their sex, which has often more time on its hands than it knows how to dispose of, from becoming idle and, therefore, vicious, that zeal for religion might be fostered, and women be enabled to exercise and develop their higher sensibilities which would otherwise languish.

During the great *pujáhs* which consume so much of our means, women are left in the background. Their special province is these ceremonies, *Vratas*, as they are called. Each has a *Kathá* or tale tacked on to it, which is piously recited by the most elderly of the assembled female worshippers. Each story is illustrative of the might and glory of the particular god or goddess that is being honoured and in itself forms a highly interesting part of the ceremony. Most of the tales may seem to unbelievers to be as wild and childish as nursery legends, yet they are delightful. They please less by the variation of "moving accidents" than by the homeliness of their construction. They are extremely interesting also for the light they throw on the recesses of the Indian woman's heart.

I may here add that the performance of these ceremonies is believed to bring with it a reward which is in consistence with the special attributes of the deity worshipped. Some of the observances secure the safety and well-being of the worshipper's children; and some the beatitude consequent on devotion to one's husband. Many of these tales have obvious morals attached to them and they all end with exhortations calling upon the devout hearers to follow the example of the hero or heroine of the narrative. The observances are finished with profound bows on all sides to the deities, accompanied by shrill cries of "*ulu—ulu—ulu*" which are considered auspicious and are peculiar to the fair sex.

My main object being to narrate the tales as they are recited, I have dismissed the rituals with scanty notice, only mentioning such facts as have struck me as specially interesting. The compilation, it is hoped, will give an insight into the domestic life of our women in one of its highest bearings. There is not a week in the year which does not bring with it some holy festival. The orthodox Hindu's life is, indeed, one round of ceremonies, observances, fasts, and festivals: and this is emphatically true of Hindu women. Married life and widowhood abound in such duties, and they form the tendrils that hold together the ancient faith inculcated by *Pauránic Hinduism*.

The foreign reader may, perchance, find amusement in these faint echoes from an unknown world. If studiously inclined, he may trace curious and far-reaching analogies between the traditions and ceremonies of our women-folk and those of other nations of the world, past and present.

D. N. NEOGI.

CONTENTS

LIST OF ILLUSTRATIONS

SACRED TALES OF INDIA.

I.

THE MANASA OR NÁGA-PANCHAMI CEREMONY.

[This *Puják* is performed on the last day of *Áshádh* which falls in July. The deities are the goddess *Manasá* or *Padmá*, the daughter of Siva and wife of Jaratkáru, and her offspring, the snake-king Ananta and his four brothers. It is a worship of snakes—a relic, perhaps, of the faith of the aborigines of India—who have also bequeathed to us the legacy of stone and tree-worship, and swelled the Hindu pantheon with such deities as Jarásura, the god of fevers, Sitalá, the goddess of small-pox, etc. Padmá and her reptilian brood are worshipped towards the beginning of the rains, as it is in that season that, a great part of the country being submerged, all dry places and dwellings of men in villages are infested by this dreadful scourge of man. Manasá is sometimes worshipped in an image described as follows in the *Devi Purána*: She is as charming as the moon and adorned with pearls and with such jewels as are to be found on the heads of snakes, is generally represented as being mounted on a drake, and attended by the eight chief snakes.]

THE TALE.

The Divine Brothers.

KRISIDHAN, a rich farmer, had seven sons, all of whom were married. One cold and rainy day their seven wives went for a bath in a tank near by and fell to talking as to what each of them would best enjoy on such a day. The eldest said she could wish for nothing better than to be at her father's house, have a good meal of fish and meat, and after a really good sleep wake up again as hungry as before. The second thought that the best thing one could wish for on such a day was also to be at one's father's house, to have plenty of sweetmeat and cakes to eat, and to be sitting or lounging in idleness the whole day long. And so on. All the six wives had each her say excepting the seventh —the youngest. She kept silent whilst the others were talking, until at last one, noticing that she looked sad, asked her,

"Sister, why don't you also tell us what you would wish for? We have all had our turn. Now it is yours."

"Sister," cried she in reply, "each of you has a father and a father's house to go to and has wished to be there eating and sleeping according to your fancy; but you know, sister, I have nowhere to go, nor have I relations elsewhere. So who is there to gratify my wishes?"

"But, sister," said the former, "merely wishing will not give us what we want; our chances are no better than yours; all this is mere idle talk to keep our tongues agoing."

"If that be so," rejoined Lahaná, for that was the name of the youngest wife, "I will not disappoint you. On such a day as this my wish would be to have a good meal of *kol* fish with not a stroke of work to do the whole day long."

When they had bathed and filled each one her pitcher, on their way homeward, Lahaná who was a little ahead of the company espied in a small pool, no bigger than the space covered by a cow's hoof, two *kol* fishes splashing about merrily. One of her sisters-in-law coming up cried out gaily,

"Here, my sisters, we all wished in vain, for we wished too speedily; whereas Lahaná, who took her time about it, seems likely to have her wish granted, for is not here as good a pair of *kol* fishes as one could wish for?"

"Lahaná," said the eldest coming up, "take them with you in your cloth, my girl. As it is your turn both to-day and this whole month to cook, you will have an opportunity of cooking and eating them when the family meal is over."

And so Lahaná carried the fish home in her *sadi*.

Now it so happened that these two fishes were not fishes at all, but two divine serpents—Ahiráj and Maniráj—who, from a mere whim, had thus transformed themselves in order that they might test Lahaná's courage. When the general meal was over, Lahaná remembered her *kol* fishes and went to fetch them from under the cover of a basket in a corner of the kitchen

But in the meantime the fishes, who had no wish to be spiced, cooked, and eaten, had re-assumed their real shape and awaited Lahaná's arrival anxious to see what effect the sight of them would have upon her. The girl, as was to be expected, started back in surprise, but did not lose her presence of mind, and being naturally of a tender and pious turn of mind, rightly guessed that there was hidden magic in fishes which changed into snakes. As the reptiles showed no disposition to harm her, she had sufficient confidence to take them in her hand and place them in an empty cooking vessel in which she fed them regularly with milk and plantains every day. This she did for a month; and when her turn of officiating at the kitchen was ended, one of her six sisters-in-law took her place. Her successor did not know that the snakes were in the cooking vessel until by chance she raised the cover, when they hissed and darted forward, perceiving that a stranger had come.

"What snake-charmer's daughter have we got in the house," cried the young woman in horror, "who cherishes snakes in a cooking vessel and will have some of us, poor creatures, bitten and killed one of these days ?"

After this Lahaná removed them to the store-house where the corn was kept and fed them there. And when, after a month or so, her mother-in-law went into the granary to fetch some corn, the snakes, knowing that it was not Lahaná, hissed and darted forward as they had done before.

"Who is it that keeps snakes in a granary ? She must surely belong to a family of snake-charmers, and we, poor creatures, who have not her skill will be bitten and killed one of these days ?" gasped she, falling back terrified. Lahaná again removed her charges, and continued to feed and nourish them as before until a time came when food was no longer plentiful and she could get neither milk nor plantains. So she took them to a neighbouring field and saying,

"Dear creatures, whom I scarcely know by what name to call, I am a poor woman—a dependant on others. I find it now beyond my means to feed you any longer. It behoves you, therefore, to go your way and do me and mine no harm," she placed them on a sod and came away.

The snakes were, as the reader already knows, divine beings, sons of the goddess Manasá or Padmá. On hearing what Lahaná said they returned to their home in the nether world. Arrived there they went at once like spoilt children to their mother.

"Mother," said they, "we have had strange adventures on earth." They then related the whole story of how they had turned themselves into *kol* fishes and had been taken home by Lahaná, and how they had re-assumed their proper shapes when on the point of being cooked and eaten, and had been fed and nourished by her for a whole year.

"Now, mother," added they, "it beseems us to do something in return for this daughter of man. She has been very kind and devoted to us, and if she had any food left to give us would not have sent us away. We know she has no relations in her father's family to give her a welcome home for a change and holiday. We would we could get her here when we should act towards her as if we were her brothers, and as for you, you could fill the place of a mother to her."

"My darlings," replied she, "you ask me to do what is extremely difficult. You are divine and she is human. How can there be an alliance or any close intercourse between her and you? But I would not interfere with such a generous wish. You may fetch her here. If she is not more than pleased with her new relations, I shall not be to blame for it."

The two brothers, Ahiráj and Maniráj, highly delighted set out again for the earth; and when they arrived near the house of the farmer, put on the disguise of two young men and in a trice were attended by a long train of servants carrying all sorts of presents of eatables and silken apparel, and bearers with a palanquin to carry Lahaná, and maid-servants to attend her.

At the gate of the farmer's house they knocked,—

"Father-in-law, are you at home? Mother-in-law, are you at home? We are brothers of the wife of your youngest son and have come to see her."

At this the master and mistress of the house threw the gate open wondering who these brothers might be and where they had sprung from, as it was well known that Lahaná had no relations. But the sight of the long train of servants bearing presents quickly wrought a change in their minds. They and their good neighbours reasoned—Why should they not be her brothers? Who but they that held her near to their hearts could give such presents? And when the new-comers said that they had gone as traders to a distant country before Lahaná was born, and had been away from home ever since, and had only now returned to find her grown up and married, and had now come to take her home for a few days, they all said, "It must be as they say; they are clearly her brothers though we have never heard of them before. Were there not many things of which people knew very little yet which were perfectly true?"

They then welcomed the brothers and the sight of the presents gladdened their hearts. Lahaná had her misgivings, but she did not allow her tongue to utter what passed in her mind. After the midday meal had been eaten, Ahiráj and Maniráj obtained permission from the farmer to take her with them for a few days; and at the first favourable opportunity they started on their journey.

The three—two divine and one human—after wending their way at a rapid rate, now stood on the shore of a great lake. They were only three, for the long train of servants had melted into thin air when a few miles from the farmer's house. Ahiráj and Maniráj now explained matters, saying,

"Child of mortals, you have possibly guessed by this time that we are not of your species; we are divine and sons of Padmá Ráni. We it was whom, in the shape of snakes, you nourished with milk and plantains; and we mean to repay you for your goodness to us. Consider us as your brothers, for like brothers we shall love and reward you."

Saying this they changed themselves into snakes, and bidding Lahaná hold fast by their tails plunged into the water. They had previously taken care to blindfold her with a piece of cloth so that she might not see the dreadful sights that would otherwise have presented themselves to her view. They then swam to the middle of the lake and dived headlong down, Lahaná holding tightly to them. She heard weird sounds and was aware of the most peculiar sensations; but she did not see anything. When at last this strange journey came to an end, and the bandage on her eyes was removed, she found she was in a country where everything was strange. In reply to her questions her pretended brothers told her it was their country.

"Sister," said they, "when we take you home, you will find our mother lying on a couch of gold with her feet upon a foot-stool of silver and being fanned with a fan made of the white cow's hair. Salute her by prostrating yourself on the ground before her."

She promised to obey; and on her presentation to the goddess shortly afterwards, did as she had been instructed.

Lahaná had not been in the abode of Padmá Ráni for a week, before the time came for the goddess to go down to the earth to enjoy the *pujáhs* that would be offered her. On the eve of her departure she called Lahaná to her side and desired her to keep the house in her absence.

"Lahaná," she said, "every day in the morning as soon as the milkman and the fruiterer have brought in their loads, boil the milk, and peel the fruits, and mix them, and pour a quantity into each of these holes wherein live my children. Do not forget this, and do not be at any time too sure of your own safety."

Now it so happened that on the second day of the goddess's absence from home, when the milkman and the fruiterer had brought the milk and plantains, and the time had come for Lahaná to bestir herself, she slept the sleep of the dead. Presently she woke with a start and saw the serpent brood of her adopted mother darting forward, hissing loudly all the time, from the crevices in the floor and the walls. Quickly kindling a fire she boiled the milk, and mixing crushed plantains in it, poured a quantity of the burning liquid into each of the holes, without a thought of the rashness and folly of what she did. Plainly her action was more likely to result in the death of the serpents than to satisfy their hunger. Some of the snakes had their heads, some their tongues, some their eyes, and some their tails scalded or burnt, and furious with pain they hissed and glared. Some of them were for killing Lahaná instantly, and others for waiting only till their mother should return. But Karkat Nág, the youngest of Padmá Ráni's sons, and the most ill-tempered of them all, darted from his hiding place and struck his fangs into Lahaná, who fell dead on the ground. where they covered her with a basket.

Meantime the goddess Padmá Ráni, seated in her temple on earth, felt her throne being violently shaken. It boded ill; and using her divine powers she soon found out how matters stood at her house. So, hurriedly finishing the business on hand, she quickly repaired to her home in the nether region.

Scarcely had she set her foot on the threshold of her house before a hundred angry voices were up. Cries and groans were mixed with complaints of what Lahaná had done. The goddess calmed them all with soothing words, and healed their burns by passing her hand over the affected parts. She took Karkat Nág severely to task for being so vengeful, and bathed the lifeless Lahaná in nectar who, thereupon, returned to life. As soon as this was done, Padmá Ráni turned to her children and smiled.

"Children," said she, "we have had enough of our human alliance. It is time the daughter of man was sent back to her earthly home before further evil befalls her."

They acquiesced. But they decided not to bedeck the whole of her person with jewels, as is the custom, but only half of it because of the injuries she had done them. When every preparation was made for the journey, the goddess called Lahaná to her side, and caressing her head said,

"Lahaná, these children of mine are not, as you have seen, the meekest of creatures, so you should be advised as to how to bear yourself with regard to them. Let me tell you that when Ahiráj and Maniráj have taken you home, they will remain near you, although you will not be able to see them, to hear what you say of them. So touch your mother-in-law's feet with that one of yours whereon you have worn the *mal* (bangles) when she comes to take you out of the palanquin; and when she cries in disgust—'Ha, daughter, had you not better reserve your vanity for the day when they shall set off the whole of your person with gold instead of only half of it?'—say in reply, 'Long life to mother Padmá Ráni, mother-in-law, and to brothers Ahiráj and Maniráj. If I have got ornaments only on half of my body this time, I shall have them on the other half by and by.'"

And she promised to obey her.

She then set out with her adopted brothers, and by the same way and through the same wide lake they journeyed till they came within a few miles of the farmer's house. At this point Ahiráj and Maniráj changed themselves into two young men, as before, and placed Lahaná in a palanquin. Attended by a long train of servants bearing rich presents, the brothers accompanied her until all the party reached the gate of the farmer's house when they knocked crying,

"Father-in-law, are you at home? Mother-in-law, are you at home? We are brothers of the wife of your youngest son come to return her."

Presently the gate was opened. The mother-in-law came forward to receive Lahaná, and she in dismounting touched her feet with that one of hers on which there was the *mal*; whereon the mother-in-law cried in disgust,

"Ha, daughter, had you not better reserve your vanity for the day when they shall set off the whole of your person with gold instead of only half of it?"

And Lahaná, as instructed, replied,

"Long life to mother Padmá Ráni, O mother-in-law,

and to brothers Ahiráj and Maniráj. If I have got ornaments on only half of my body this time, I shall have them on the other half by and by."

Ahiráj and Maniráj, who, though invisible, were close by, were much pleased at this reply, for it showed that though they had not used her quite well inasmuch as they had bedecked only half her person, she bore them no spite ; nay, wished them long life.

When they returned home, they said as much to their mother, and added—

"We must get Lahaná here again for a few days so that we may remove the slight we have done her in adorning only half her body. It is a good girl, mother, that does not speak ill even of those who have done her ill."

The goddess approving, they set out again for the earth. Very rich presents gladdened the hearts of the farmer and his wife, and they did not object to Lahaná's going with her so-called brothers a second time. The few days that she spent in their home this time passed without any mishap, and she was bedecked with jewels over her whole body and not over half only as before. Padmá Ráni who was always her well-wisher gave her some parting instructions before she left in company of Ahiráj and Maniráj, who, as before, were to take her back to her earthly home.

As soon as Lahaná had dismounted from her palanquin into the loving embrace of her mother-in-law, she, in compliance with the instructions she had received, scattered a handful of paddy on the courtyard and picking them up, inquired of a neighbour,

"Sister, how fares he who turns good to evil ?"

And the neighbour answered,

"He is burnt to ashes, sister, who turns good to evil."

And lo! there fell from the air above two small handfuls of ashes at Lahaná's feet. She knew them to be the remains of Ahiráj and Maniráj who, unseen by all, had been waiting to overhear what might be said of them. Padmá Ráni had taught Lahaná the words of a charm, which she had no sooner pronounced than the serpents sprang back to life and bade her adieu for good.

Ahiráj and Maniráj had not gone far before they fell to conversing with each other.

"Maniráj," said his brother, "this child of man, Lahaná, must be an exceptionally good girl. When we were reduced to ashes by the decree of a relentless fate, she gave us back our life. But we have not as yet done much for her; let us be more liberal."

And they put their heads together and hit upon a plan. Making their way to the palace of the king of the country, they bit to death the young prince—his only son. Oh! what wailing there was, what a tempest of grief, what confusion, and what running far and near in search of snake-doctors. In the meantime, Ahiráj and Maniráj had disguised themselves as two old Bráhmans, and were walking leisurely about the palace. They inquired, as if they did not know, of those who were running to and from the palace what the trouble was, and what unsettled them; and on being told the reason, they said they were snake-doctors, and were confident that they could cure the prince in no time. In a minute they were carried into the presence of the king.

"Great king," said they, "we will cure your son on one condition. It is that you will adopt the wife of the youngest son of the farmer, Krisidhan, living in your territory, as a daughter of your own house, and that you will treat her in every way as such—fetching her to your palace, and entertaining her right royally from time to time, and heaping upon her and her relations this world's goods of which you have so large a share and they so little."

The king, of course, readily promised to do all this and more ; and Ahiráj and Maniráj drew out the venom they had instilled into the prince's body. He got up as if after a refreshing sleep. There was now great rejoicing, and song and laughter flowed.

Thus did Ahiráj and Maniráj provide a father's house for the fatherless Lahaná, who was henceforth frequently sent for and welcomed to the palace, and treated as a daughter of the royal house. She enjoyed the sweets of such a high connection for many a long year, all, it must be remembered, by favour of Padmá Ráni. And when she was dead, she was driven to heaven in a chariot of light, also through the intercession of the same goddess.

So, ye all that have listened to this sacred *kathá*, cry victory to Manasá ;—*ulu ! ulu ! ulu !*

II.

THE SÁVITRI CEREMONY.

[Sávitri is not a goddess. She does not trace her lineage to any deity. She has been deified on account of her eminent virtues and is worshipped in the month of May on the fourteenth day after the full moon. She is described in the Mahábhárata as a charming young damsel who, though a princess, voluntarily betook herself to a life of severe austerities in a forest. Afterwards she resumed her station in her palace and departing from this world, when the time was ripe, attained to beatitude. Our women worship her for fourteen years at a stretch, once a year. An earthen jar is placed at the foot of a banyan tree and the spirit of Sávitri is supposed to animate it. Only married women perform this ceremony; and if successfully performed, they never lose their husbands even as Sávitri herself did not.]

THE TALE.

Snatched from Death.

KING ASVAPATI of Ujjayinee belonged to the Solar race of monarchs. His vast dominions which comprised seas and islands had no joy for him, for though he had taken to himself a wife for over a score of years, the union had not been blessed with any children. He performed the great *Putreshti* sacrifice to the gods in the hope of being blessed with a child and impatiently awaited the result. The gods seemed to listen to his prayers, for the queen conceived and was in due time brought to bed of a charming daughter. The king named her Sávitri. As Sávitri grew up, the delight of her parents, she received such education as befitted her sex and rank. Soon the time came when her royal father thought of marrying her, but he could not find an eligible youth. At last he gave her liberty to choose her own husband, and as a result she visited cities and hermitages attended only by her maids.

In one of these trips she met a handsome youth, the son, presumably, of a hermit, and was smitten with love at first sight. This was Satyabán, who in his turn was also smitten by passion. But they both chose to keep their feelings to themselves. A few months later, king Asvapati, under the impression that his daughter had not yet met with anyone whom she could love, called a council of the elders of his court for consultation as to the desirability of holding a regular *svayamvara*, or ceremony of self-choice to which young princes from all the states of Bháratbarsha should be invited. He felt that Sávitri could not fail to find a husband worthy of her love among so many guests. These grave councillors had not been long in the council-hall, before Sávitri, who had guessed their purpose, came, like the prudent girl she was, to set them right.

"Father," said she, addressing the king, "you need not think of a *svayamvara*, for I am already more a married woman than a maid. Start not, my lord. You have heard of and seen Satyabán, the son of the hermit. It is he who is the chosen companion of my life here and hereafter. It is he, father, who occupies my heart fully—there is no room for another!"

Now the king and his grave councillors were in a pretty fix. How could a princess be married to the son of a hermit? Bred in the lap of every conceivable luxury she could not endure the life of an ascetic. Besides, would the hermit allow his son to marry beneath his caste?

But to help them out of this difficulty, who should knock at the door just at that moment but Nárada himself, the celestial hermit, son of Brahmá, the grandsire of all the universe?

After he had been received with the customary *Pádya*[1] and *Arghya*[1] and been conducted to a seat of deer-skin with the deepest reverence such as was due to him, the question was referred to him for solution. Nárada to whom nothing was unknown said,

"O King, when you have heard my story you will agree that Sávitri had better live single than unite herself to Satyabán. For this Satyabán is no son of a hermit; the old, blind man, his father, who wears an ascetic's garb, is none other than king Dyumatsena himself reduced to this strait by the enemies of his house. He was met in the field, conquered, and driven from his throne and palace. Here you see him now. But what concerns you most," continued the celestial sage, "is that there is a terrible curse upon Satyabán, and he is fated to die within a year of his marriage."

Sávitri shuddered involuntarily at this, but quickly regained her self-possession.

"Reverend father," said she addressing Nárada, "if it is to be as you say, let it be. As for me, I am at this moment a widow if you resolve I am not to marry him. I cannot marry another, for that would be a sin. One can elect a husband but once, not twice. In my heart

[1] Water to wash the feet with and a present of honey, *ghee*, curd, milk, etc.

I have given myself to him. Let me also tell you that I can bear widowhood for eternity after having Satyabán as my husband for a day."

Upon this, and after some further deliberation, it was determined that Sávitri should wed the beloved of her heart.

The scene now shifts to the forest—to the hermitage of Dyumatsena, where Sávitri and Satyabán, who were now wedded, lived. Sávitri made an exemplary wife and an affectionate daughter-in-law, in spite of having discarded every luxury and comfort to which she had been accustomed. She was the stay of her father-in-law and mother-in-law in their old age, and made Satyabán so happy that he did not feel the loss of a prospective throne. He, it may be mentioned. did not know that a heavy curse was hanging over him, and Sávitri did not wish to make her husband unhappy with the foretaste of death.

Month after month passed quickly away ; and at last the time came when it wanted but a day to the date on which his doom had been foretold.

Sávitri had passed the whole day in worshipping the gods as, indeed, she had done all through the year, praying to them to avert the terrible decree. When she retired to bed at night, she begged Satyabán to take her with him on the following morning in his daily excursion into the woods for fruits, roots, and sacred fuel. He wondered much at the unusual request, but consented to comply with her wish.

On the following morning, the loving couple went together into the depths of the forest. Sávitri followed her husband like a shadow, and when he climbed up a tree to pluck fruits, she stood beneath with her eyes fixed on him, for there was no knowing at what particular moment the curse, like the sword of Damocles, might fall on her dear husband's head.

Satyabán was not many minutes aloft, when he felt a severe headache. Coming hastily down and unable to support himself, he fell prone on the ground at his wife's feet. Although the shock to Sávitri was a great one, yet it was not one for which she was altogether unprepared, for, as the reader is aware, a dread catastrophe had long been foretold to her. Satyabán was not, however, dead. "Sávitri, my darling," gasped he, "I am dying. O, what a pain there is in my head! Let it rest on your knees—Sávitri, my darling!" The next minute all was over.

Sávitri wept not. With the dear remains of her lord in her arms, she sat there, a statue of grief, watching what might follow. It was in a happy age when wonderful things were wont to happen. No sooner had Satyabán breathed his last than the messengers of Yama, the king of the dead, came down to take their victim to his place in the other world. But the chastity that hedged in the person of the wife was as a burning flame, and those grim messengers did not dare approach her for fear of being consumed by it. They returned to their master saying, "Lord, we cannot." Yama was astonished, but resolved to see for himself what it all meant. So, armed with his club, robed in scarlet, and mounting on his favourite buffalo, the dread deity set off to where Sávitri held her dead husband in her embrace. Yama himself felt her influence and he, too, was struck with awe. He did not, however, shrink from his duty, but gently approaching the damsel, "Daughter Sávitri," said he in his softest voice, "I am here to take your husband away; he is mine now. You, I suppose, know who I am."

"I know you by your words," replied she gently but firmly, "you are Yama. My husband may now be your property, and so will I be too; you can take him, but not without me."

"How can that be?" cried the dread visitor. "Such is not my mission; you must part with your husband, girl. The living cannot accompany the dead."

"You cannot persuade me of that," returned Sávitri, holding the corpse tighter in her embrace.

Yama was struck by the devotion of the young wife, and, anxious to do what he could for her, said, "Sávitri, you may keep your husband's body, and as I am exceedingly pleased with you, I wish to give you aught you may wish for except one thing, that is the life of your husband."

"If you are pleased, great Lord of the dead, and will grant me a boon, kindly let my father who has no son have one who will live to hand down his name to posterity."

"It shall be so," said the other, "but go home now, for it is not well to stay here alone."

So saying, he turned his back upon her and, taking with him the soul of Satyabán, proceeded on his journey. A few minutes after, he looked back, thinking of the poor faithful wife. Lo! she was at his heels.

"Whither art thou going?" cried he in surprise. "What good is there in following me, child? Go home."

"Go home?" replied Sávitri quietly. "Whither my lord goes I go. I have no home but where he is. O King of the dead, you know a true wife follows her husband through life and death. A god though you be, you cannot stop me."

And Yama, who was greatly affected, said, "Sávitri, ask for still another boon excepting, of course, the life of your husband and you shall have it."

Sávitri replied, "If you are pleased, dread god, let my father-in-law, king Dyumatsena, recover his lost kingdom and his sight."

You must know, gentle reader, that the poor old man had not only been driven from his throne, but had also been blinded by his enemies.

"He shall," answered Yama, "and now go your way home, and let me go mine."

He held on and lessened not his pace until, out of curiosity, he turned his head once again to see if Sávitri was out of sight.

Sávitri was still close behind him!

"Sávitri, why are you following me?" exclaimed Yama, unable to suppress his surprise.

"I cannot choose but do so," was her calm reply, "you have in your possession all that I hold dear in heaven and on earth; and, besides, you are so good and kind. Why should I stay behind?"

"My girl," said Yama, his heart melting with pity, "I would give you your husband back, if I could; but ask for a third boon, and if it be not the life of Satyabán, it shall be given thee."

Whereupon said Sávitri with folded hands, "Great God, as you have so far granted every request of your poor supplicant, grant me that I may have a hundred sons by Satyabán, each born after an interval of a hundred years!"

"It shall be so," said Yama thoughtlessly, bent only

upon pleasing his fair petitioner and upon inducing her to leave him alone.

Then Sávitri stood right across Yama's path and smilingly said, " Let me have my husband ! "

" How now ? " cried Yama. " You are unreasonable, child."

" Unreasonable ? Indeed, I am not," answered Sávitri gaily. "Consider the boon you have last granted me and say if it can be accomplished without your returning me my Satyabán."

Yama perceived the truth of what she said, and was conquered, as he had never been before ; and that too by a girl. But she was strong by virtue of her undying love, her pious and self-sacrificing devotion. Yama yielded his charge not unwillingly, in that it gave the world an example to follow. And Sávitri returned home with her husband, rejoicing.

Her father-in-law was now no longer a hermit and her husband, a hermit's son. The old man had regained his sight and, with it, his kingdom. But the cares of a kingdom are a sore weight to one in the shady vale of life and who has, moreover, tasted the calm of a hermit's life. It was not long before he resigned his crown in favour of his son Satyabán who mounted the throne of his fathers with Sávitri, a queen who was to be for ever glorious because of her undying love and chastity.

So, ye all that have listened to this sacred *kathá*, cry victory to Sávitri, and may ye all be even as she was ;— *ulu ! ulu ! ulu !*

III.

THE ITU CEREMONY.

[This ceremony is performed on the four Sundays intervening between the last days of Kártic and Agraháyan—November and December of the English calendar. The god is represented by a small earthen jar upon a flat dish of the same material and with a lid covering its mouth. Blades of grass, unhusked paddy, and vermilion are. amongst other offerings, indispensable. This, like all other religious ceremonies, has to be performed fasting.]

THE TALE.

By Itu's Favour.

A BRÁHMAN who lived upon charity had a wife and two daughters. It was in the winter month of December when it was the custom to eat cakes, that, as the mendicant moved from door to door, he saw everyone enjoying the tasty morsels. Poor Bráhmans, in general, are well known for their huge appetites; and beggar though he was, our Bráhman was a prince of gluttons. His mouth watered at the sight of those goodly cakes, and returning home, he entreated his wife to bake him some. In reply he received a torrent of feminine eloquence: "For shame, man, how can you talk of eating cakes, when you have scarcely enough to feed a dog on?" Poverty does not tend to make wives either sweet-tongued or sweet-tempered. The Bráhman was stung to the quick, and resolved to procure the materials for a few cakes. Extending his round of mendicancy from half-a-dozen to about nine villages, he succeeded in getting a quantity of wheat, and sugar, a little *ghee*, and half a cocoanut. These he brought to his wife. But as he was handing them to her, a portion was blown away by the wind, and a portion fell on the dusty earth and was lost. Giving her what was left, he gave strict injunctions that neither she nor either of his daughters were to take even a nibble at the dainties which she was to prepare; and if they did, he said, he would not scruple to banish them from his sight for ever. Now it so happened that the good wife, anxious to keep the matter secret from her daughters, resolved to bake the cakes at night when they were asleep. Getting to know of this, the Bráhman, who was suspicious of his wife, determined to keep a watch, and taking a piece of string hid himself behind the kitchen door. As soon as he heard the peculiar sound which announced that a cake was baked, he tied a knot in the string, thus keeping an account of how many cakes were made.

In the meantime, the elder daughter had been awakened by the savoury smell of the cakes and, getting up, begged to have one, which the mother, not finding it in her heart to refuse, gave her.

Shortly afterwards the second daughter got up and said, "Pray, mamma, let me have one; I am so hungry."

She too had one, and by this time the cooking was over.

Next morning, the dish was laid before the Bráhman who, without waiting to perform his ablutions or say his prayers, took it and sat down with his back to the sun. He had the string with the knots in his left hand; with the right he counted the cakes. They were two short of the proper number.

"Now, where are the other two, wife?" roared the infuriated Bráhman. The woman said his daughters had eaten them. Their fate was sealed.

A few days afterwards, the Bráhman called his daughters to him and said—

"Girls, would you like to visit your uncle's home? Go, pack up, and we will go."

Now Ramá, the younger girl, had heard from her mother of the sinister design of her inhuman father, and she warned her sister, Isáni, what the trip to their uncle's really meant. But they could not help themselves, and accordingly set out with their father, who had equipped himself with a conch-shell, a lock of hair, and some bits of *áltá* (coloured cotton) which were dyed blood-red. The party then started off, the two daughters following their father, until, towards evening, they entered a great forest. When they had gone some way through it, the girls, weary and footsore, felt sleepy and told their father so. The Bráhman told them to lie down on the grass and gave them two bricks to serve as pillows. As soon as they were fast asleep the Bráhman pounded the conch-shell which he had brought with him, and whitened the ground with the powder. He then scattered the bits of *áltá* on the ground and with them the hair which he had with him. His object in doing this was to make his daughters believe that he had been attacked and killed by some wild beast. Having made all these preparations, he speedily disappeared.

It was not long before the girls awoke, and called, and sought for their father in vain. They wept, and their tears gave them some relief. The shades of evening were falling fast, and the time soon came for those denizens of the forest that are most unfriendly to man to show themselves. Snakes, large and small, hissed amidst the grass; elephants and rhinoceroses crushed through trees and thickets; tigers prowled about for what they might devour, while the lion in all his majesty held court in the forest which, to the consternation of the lesser beasts, shook with his mighty roaring. Now, too, cannibals began to search every nook and corner of the woods for unfortunate woodmen who had lost themselves and become separated from their companions. The girls, filled with terror, knew not what to do. At last, slowly approaching a large Açwattha tree that stood towering above all other trees as if it were the monarch of the forest, they addressed it, saying,

"O tree, pity us unfortunate beings! Thou knowest our danger. Give us shelter within thy heart this night!"

Thus appealed to, the tree took compassion on the girls and forthwith its trunk slowly opened, showing a spacious cavern within. The girls quickly entered the opening when the tree closed of itself. The wild animals, scenting the presence of human beings, began to tear at the tree, and growl, and roar around it, but it was impossible for them to get at the girls, who were so safely hidden within the heart of that monarch of the forest. Thus the Bráhman's daughters passed the night, and when morning came, they once more prayed to the tree, saying,

"O tree, thou hast saved our life. It is morning now, and do thou open thyself so that we may get out!"

The tree, hearing the prayer, opened itself wide, and the sisters came out. They prostrated themselves before their protector and then set out along a narrow path leading, they knew not whither. Soon they came to the outskirts of a village where some damsels of exquisite beauty were performing religious rites. The sisters sat at some distance and watched the proceedings. One of the group took notice of the forlorn-looking girls and kindly asked them what they wanted. The poor souls faltered out their sad tale. The young woman then said compassionately,

"Why don't you, like us, worship Itu Thákur? You would then have nothing to complain of. Great wealth, a goodly race of children, learning, fame—everything would be yours and your sire's and children's. Itu Thákur will give you all."

The girls were eager to begin. The young woman and some of her companions supplied them with the *pujáh* requisites, which consisted of a small earthen jar, painted red with vermilion, an earthen dish, a lid of the same material for the jar, some unhusked paddy, and a few blades of grass. The girls were first asked to wash themselves in a large lake not far from where they were. They proceeded in the direction pointed out, but when they came to the side of the lake, lo, the water had all dried up! The fish were gasping and struggling in the moist earth, the water fowl were uttering plaintive cries, and the lotus stalks were languishing for want of water, whilst on the shores the washermen and women stood still, and the bathers stood in crowds filled with disappointment at being deprived of their daily bath. The *rishis*,[1] too, could no longer offer their oblations to the

[1] Hermits.

deities. Everybody was filled with amazement and set himself to ascertain the cause of so extraordinary an occurrence. At last the cause was discovered. The two girls had never before worshipped Itu, and the deity had been offended by the scant ceremony which had been paid him. Ashamed of what had happened, the maidens came back to the worshippers and told them what had happened. The ladies took pity on them and gave them a ring of sacred hay. The girls took it and threw it, according to their instructions, into the empty lake, when, at once, it became filled with water as before! The fish began to swim again, the water fowl circled round uttering cries of pleasure, the washermen and their wives resumed their task of beating the cloths they sought to wash, the crowds of bathers joyously plunged into the water, and the *rishis* finished their oblations to the deities. The two girls then bathed and came back. After which they worshipped the god with the sincerity of guileless hearts. And he in his turn seemed to be highly gratified; for, presently, a voice spoke to them from above:

"What is the chief desire of your hearts, O daughters of man?"

With folded hands they answered,

"Let us be in comfortable circumstances; let our father have wealth and a son, kind god!"

Their prayers were granted, and the girls continued to live in that village in comfort and devoutly worshipped the god.

Some years later, Isáni and Ramá remembered their parents and their old home and set out to revisit them. Meanwhile, their father, by virtue of their piety, had grown immensely rich. Their mother often thought of them and wept over the memory of her loved ones. So, when some of the neighbours ran to her one day and exclaimed, "Your daughters Isáni and Ramá have come back," she would not believe them, but said, "Miserable creature that I am, shall I ever see them again on earth? It is long, neighbours, long since they were removed from the busy paths of life—poor, dear girls!"

Conceive, then, her surprise, her boundless joy when her long-lost Isáni and Ramá presented themselves before her in the flesh. The first outbursts of joy and grief, of smiles and tears over, the whole family settled down to the common-place cares of life. The Bráhman, now partly reconciled to his daughters, prospered steadily because of their piety, though he was ignorant of how deeply he was indebted to them.

In about a year's time, the king of the country gave a very splendid feast at his palace to which princes and learned Bráhmans from all quarters of the globe were invited; and it was proclaimed through all the country by beat of golden tom-toms that whoever, on that occasion, should discuss the *Shástras* best, should be rewarded with half a kingdom. Pundits flocked to the palace from all parts; but Isáni's father would not go. Ramá noticed it, and addressing him, said, "Father, why do you not answer the invitation of the king?"

He replied, "I am not well versed in the *Shástras*. What business is it of yours whether I go or not?"

"Nay, but, father," mildly rejoined Ramá, "if you do but go to the palace, I may, perchance, put you in the way of gaining half a kingdom."

"How can you?"

"Depend upon me, I can. As to the how, you will see by and by."

The Bráhman was willing to go on that understanding. That day Ramá worshipped the Thákur, and in answer to her prayers was promised that her father should excel in *Shástric* discussions at the court and carry off the prize.

Now it so happened that the Bráhman had always been notorious for being a dunce, and the assembled pundits could scarcely keep still when they saw him taking his seat in their ranks. But judge of their surprise when, during the discussions, learned *slokas* and weighty arguments fell from his lips in rapid succession. They were forced to confess that Saraswati, the goddess of all learning, sat enthroned on his tongue. Ramá's promise was fulfilled, and to the Bráhman was awarded the promised half kingdom. But no sooner had he left the court than he forgot his learning, and when, at the gate of the palace a pundit asked him to solve a knotty question, he had not a word to answer and was called a fortunate ass and laughed at by the bystanders. This made him so wretched that even the prize of half a kingdom brought him no solace. He was very angry with his daughter who had sent him to court; and malicious creature that he was, he once again resolved to put the two poor girls out of his way. So calling his whole family together, he swore by an image of the god Náráyana which he held in hand, that he would marry Isáni and Ramá to the two men he should first look upon on the following morning. Then he went to bed in a very bad humour.

Now, it had happened that a young prince and the son of his father's prime minister had, while returning from a hunting excursion, missed their way near the Bráhman's house and, unknown to anybody, taken up their quarters in an outhouse of his. They had bestirred themselves early, and on the Bráhman coming out, they saluted him and politely asked to be excused for having entered his house uninvited. The Bráhman started and inquired who they were, and whether they wished to wed. The latter part of the question naturally filled them with amazement, and the new-comers were struck dumb with confusion. The prince replied,

"I am a prince, and my companion is the son of my father's prime minister. We were benighted last evening and took shelter in your house, I confess, without permission. But— "

"But will you marry? That is the question. If you will, I have two grown-up daughters who are, some people say, beautiful. I am, at this moment, ready to make them over to you, prince or peasant whichever you be."

Just then, as chance would have it, the prince and the minister's son looked up and had a full view of the lovely Isáni and Ramá standing at a window. They had heard the sound of the conversation and were naturally very anxious to see who these persons might be to whom their father would, according to his vow, give them in marriage. The strangers were at once charmed, and both replied with eagerness that they would marry the Bráhman's daughters on whatever conditions he pleased. Thus, though the brutal father intended to plunge his daughters into misery by, perhaps, wedding them with the vilest of the vile, Itu Thákur interfered for the sake of his worshippers and made one a princess and the other the wife of a minister's son, ranks which you or I would thank our stars to secure for our best beloved daughters or sisters.

But watch the course of human folly. Isáni's head was turned by her sudden elevation. The pious girl who would not take a sip of water without worshipping Itu Thákur the first thing every morning, now threw aside the holy earthen jar and its lid which she had carried home from her residence in exile, most wickedly imagining that, as she had now attained the summit of human glory, Itu-worship was no longer her bounden duty. Ramá, however, clung to her jar and lived as devoutly as ever. So, while the one lost favour, the other was blessed by the deity. The way by which Isáni proceeded to the home of her husband, the prince, was marked by death and devastation, her attendants dying upon the road and the towns and villages through which she passed were devastated by fire for which no one could account, so that people rose denouncing her as a witch. On the other hand, Ramá's progress was as the advent of spring. The fields through which she passed suddenly grew thick with golden corn, trees blossomed and bore fruit, and people sang and laughed merrily with a sudden impulse of joy. Weddings and investitures with the sacred thread were celebrated everywhere. At one place, an old woman was weeping over a dead child. Ramá instantly dismounted from her palanquin and taking a palmful of holy water from her jar sprinkled the corpse with it, when lo! it rose up full of life and glowing with health and beauty.

When they reached their respective homes, their mothers-in-law came, according to the time-honoured custom, to receive the brides with the *baran-dálá*—a flat basket in which were a lamp, some blades of grass, unhusked paddy, vermilion, and other things. Now mark what happened. As soon as Isáni's mother-in-law stood before her, her *baran-dálá* together with its contents turned into iron! Ramá's mother-in-law had a different experience. No sooner had she come to her lovely daughter-in-law than her *baran-dálá* and the things it contained were converted into glittering gold! In a very short time Isáni earned an unenviable name for her baneful influence; for, before she was many months in the palace, the horses died by thousands in the royal stables, the elephants perished by hundreds, the kingdom lost province after province, and its armies were annihilated by contemptible foes. In fact, the state was on the verge of total collapse, and everyone agreed in ascribing these calamities to Isáni, who was consequently banished from the kingdom after she had given birth to a male-child whom the family-priest had named *Dukha-kumár* or the *Son of Sorrow*. Ramá, on the other hand, was adored in her new home as the very personification of Lakshmi—the goddess of good fortune. The minister rose in wealth and power as the king declined, until in time he carved out a state for himself wherein he was nearly as absolute as the king. Ramá gave birth to a son whom in joy they all agreed to call *Sukha-kumár*, or the *Son of Happiness*.

In the meantime, the old, surly Bráhman, the father of our heroines, had arranged a match for his son. While taking him and his companions to the bride's, a few miles from home, he found that the young man had forgotten to carry with him a nut-cracker, an article indispensable in marriage-rites. So, he despatched the barber who, next to the priest, is a most important person for the proper performance of the ceremonies to fetch it from home. The man, on reaching the Bráhman's house, found his mistress engaged in worshipping Itu Thákur in imitation of her daughters. She, of course, could not speak with him nor could she get up to fetch a nut-cracker, engaged, as she was, in prayer. The man returned without accomplishing his errand and laid the blame of his failure at his mistress's door. The furious Bráhman ran home, and tearing into the room where his wife sat contemplating the god with half-closed eyes, he seized the sacred jar and raising it aloft threw it with all his force on to the ground breaking it into a thousand pieces. From that moment his misfortunes began, and his downward career was rapid. His body was racked with disease; the horses in his stables perished; his elephants, and camels, and kine, and bullocks all disappeared; his wealth in land, and gold, and slaves was all gone; and finally, his once splendid mansion was reduced to his old hut with its roof of palm leaves and posts of castor stems.

Whilst this was going on a severe storm overtook the wedding party, dispersing and destroying everything, and Itu himself appeared on the scene. Armed with a stout stick of *hintal* (a close-grained wood) and with blood-red eyes, the god belaboured all the men, not sparing the bridegroom himself whom he bore through the air and cast half dead on a mound before the bride's house. Meanwhile, the bride's father and friends had waited and waited but had seen nothing of the party, and feared that the auspicious moment (*Lugna*) would pass by without the nuptial-knot being tied, in which case their family would incur great disgrace. They now began to search for the wedding party and despatched messengers far and near. They all came back unsuccessful. At last, faint groans attracted their attention, and they discovered a youth half-dead whose identity with the bridegroom was quickly established. The youth said that robbers had attacked his party and slain all his men and cast him there. He was washed and robed, and the marriage-rites were performed. The Bráhman's son made up his mind to live in his father-in-law's house unknown to his impoverished father.

Meanwhile, the Bráhman, unable to bear his distress very long and by the advice of his wife, set out for the home of his younger daughter, Ramá, where, it was hoped, he might be enriched with a few crumbs of her ample fortune. When he had reached the outskirts of her palace, he met some young women with pitchers of water on their heads. He asked them, "Whose servants are you, young women ?"

They replied, "Of Ramá Ráni, old man."

"Tell your Ráni," rejoined the wayfarer, "that there is an old Bráhman at her door who wants to see her."

He then dropped an iron pin into each of the pitchers and sat down upon the ground. The maids returned to their mistress and told her of the ancient Bráhman. But, behold ! pouring out the water from their pitchers, they found it had all been transformed into liquid gold. Whereupon Ramá cried,

"Is the old Bráhman hale or ill ? Does he look rich or poor ?"

And when they replied, "Ráni, he seemed to be very ill and in great need," she knew it was her father and instantly sent for him. He was lodged in the palace, and fed and clothed luxuriously, and taken much care of.

After a few months, the Bráhman expressed a desire to return home; and enriched with gold, jewels, and costly clothes he set out upon his journey. Ramá instructed the palanquin-bearers who were to carry him to set him down at a hut with a roof of palm-leaves and posts of castor stems, for that was his house. But the Bráhman, ashamed of owning such a poor house as that described to the bearers, bade them, when about half-way home, set him down at the gate of a very rich mansion which was not his. The bearers would not obey him and the Bráhman grew loud and haughty, but the men were obdurate. At last, he began to toss about in the palanquin in such a way that they could no longer keep it in position on their shoulders. Their patience was worn out, and they set him down and went away. They had not long gone before some ruffianly people belonging to the mansion seized him and stripped him of all his gold, and jewels, and rich clothes. He then returned to his poor wife as destitute as ever.

Some time after this, the wife in response to her husband's entreaties, started for Ramá's house to try whether she could bring home from there any money for the relief of the distress she and her husband were suffering. She was a woman and if attacked by robbers, she could secrete many things of value about her person. This was her husband's argument. In order to understand what follows it must be mentioned that since the mishap to the holy jar this woman had ceased to worship Itu. Instead of the humility which piety had inspired in her in her prosperous days, she was now, although abjectly poor, filled with vanity. Indeed, she had grown arrogant and self-willed. It was a sad trial for her pride to have to make her journey on foot and her feelings on reaching the village where her daughter lived may well be imagined. Bursting with arrogance and ill-temper she sent a message to say that she had arrived and Ramá at once despatched a palanquin and bearers, instructing the men to bring her to the back door of the mansion. But the old lady, in haughty tones, directed them to enter the mansion by the front door. Itu knew all, and, to punish the dame, broke the poles of the palanquin, just as it entered the hall where her son-in-law sat with his friends and relatives. Down she rolled on the hard floor and her cries could be heard all over the house. The scene was extremely humiliating, for many laughed outright. At last, when she was taken before her daughter, the latter upbraided her for her arrogance, but soon forgave her and made her an inmate of her house.

Whilst the events we have been relating were taking place misfortunes had been the lot of Isáni who had been banished from her husband's kingdom and had been given an asylum in Ramá's house where she lived unknown to all but her sister and mother. Isáni and her mother lived in complete forgetfulness of Itu and it naturally displeased the god to see those who held him in so little esteem treated so well, but for Ramá's sake he forebore to punish them. Meanwhile, Ramá tried her best to induce them to worship Itu. Sunday after Sunday came and went, but at *pujáh* time mother and Isáni were found to have broken their fast in the early morning and so to have become unfitted for worshipping the deity. At last one Saturday night, Ramá resolved to sleep in the same bed with them. She had their sadis tied to hers and their locks of hair also, with her own, so that they could not get up without at the same time rousing her. Towards the small hours of the morning, the god showed the most attractive variety of food to the old dame and her elder daughter. They attempted to rise and seize the food, but Ramá being disturbed and awakened, they had for very shame to lie down again. At last, the *puját* time came. The three bathed together and went through the worship. The god smiled upon Isáni and took pity on her adverse fortunes. Wealth and victory returned to her husband, the prince, and horses and elephants again filled his stables. With recovered prosperity, he began to think of his poor, banished wife and child and repented having turned them out. His troubles were owing to ill-luck —such as were foreordained; what were Isáni and her child gulity of?—so he reasoned—and calling the minister's son to him he said,

"Unless you get my wife and child back to me before the sun is down, I shall have your head cut off."

The poor man was much frightened, for he was quite ignorant of Isáni's whereabouts and felt it was not possible to trace her and get her back in a day? Surely, thought he, his days were numbered, and the sun of that day was the last that he would look upon. He came home and sat gloomily in his room, refusing food and all other creature-comforts. Ramá noticed this and asked what was the matter. When everything was told her, she said, smiling,

"You need not worry yourself on this account, my dear. Isáni is here with me, and she and her child can be restored to the prince any moment."

Meanwhile, Isáni's husband had ordered his palace to be weeded of grass and swept clean of rubbish in preparation for the return of his wife and child. Soon there came news that the procession with Isáni in it was approaching and the prince unable to restrain his eagerness hurried into the courtyard to meet her. As Isáni dismounted from her state-palanquin a blade of grass pricked her foot, and with affectation of sorrow she said,

"Alas, have I come home to be pricked with grass after such a weary exile in the heart of the forest?" When the prince heard this he was very angry and ordered the heads of the sweepers to be cut off. A short while after this, there was a grand feast at the palace. Thousands of Bráhmans and poor people were fed and clothed; and when it was nightfall and all the guests had all been served, Isáni who had been busy attending to them sat down at her meal. Hardly was the first mouthful in her mouth, when she remembered that she had not worshipped Itu Thákur that day and that it was a mortal sin to eat without previously worshipping the god, for all religious ceremonies have, as all know, to be performed before tasting food. She hastily pushed aside her dish, her heart beating loud with fear, and sent her maids in all directions to find any men or women who might not yet have broken their fast. But there was scarcely any one who had not eaten on that day of feasting. Only one poor creature, the bereaved mother of the seven sweepers whose heads had been cut off, had gone without food. She was brought before Isáni, and with her as a companion she had the *pujáh* performed. The sweeper-woman sent up her mournful prayers to the god, and it pleased him to answer her thus:

"Dig up the bodies of your sons from their graves

and bathe them with the water from the consecrated jar, and they shall come to life again."

And, in fact, as soon as the woman had carried out the god's commands her seven sons were restored to life. With golden brooms on their shoulders, they presented themselves the next day before the wondering prince to work in his palace, and from that day they grew in prosperity by favour of the god and thenceforth swept the palace and all the roads with besoms of pure gold.

Prosperity returned also to the Bráhman and his wife. The latter's residence with Ramá had, towards its close, changed her very nature and she had again become a devout worshipper of Itu. Soon after Isáni's restoration to her husband, her mother returned to her own abode and her hut disappeared, the splendid mansion that she had lived in before her husband had smashed the sacred jar taking its place. Her stables filled again; elephants, and camels, and kine multiplied. Of servants there was again a host. Gold, and jewels, and land they once more had in abundance. To crown their happiness, their son returned home with his beautiful bride.

Ramá and Isáni lived blissfully for many long years surrounded by their children and grand-children, and when their time was come, a celestial car of pure gold and decorated with thousands of tinkling bells, and *lapis-lazuli*, and gems in profusion, and hundreds of beautiful flags made of embroidered silk and other costly fabrics, descended from the sky to bear them with their husbands direct to the blissful mansions of Indra without their having to pass through the ordeal of death. They were also accompanied by their parents. The sweeper-woman too had to be taken. At her suggestion, as the car journeyed through the air, its occupants proclaimed to the wonder-stricken world below the might and glory of Itu through whose favour alone they were ascending to heaven in their own bodily forms. From that day forward the worship of Itu spread among the peoples of the earth.

So, ye all that have listened to this sacred *kathá* cry all hail to Itu Thákur ;—*ulu! ulu! ulu!*

IV.

THE BUDHÁSHTAMI CEREMONY.

[This ceremony is performed on the eighth day of the dark fortnight in any month of the year. Once begun it must be performed eight times. The goddess worshipped is Párvati, Siva's spouse. The observance of this ceremony frees the worshipper from the sin of robbing Bráhmans in particular, and from all sins in general. The worshipper is bound, during the year or years the ceremony is continued, to have eight handfuls and no more for her daily meals. It is said in the *Bramhánda Purána* that the performance of Budháshtami entitles a person to as much bliss as is earned by the bestowal of a hundred milch kine upon Bráhmans and the digging of a thousand tanks and wells for public good. It also annuls the sins committed in a hundred previous births.]

THE TALE.

The Bride of Yama, the King of the Dead.

At the village of Saûndaryapur in the kingdom of Pátaliputra there lived a poor Bráhman whose name was Bara; his wife was Rambhá, his son, Kaûsik, and his daughter, Bijayá. Now Kaûsik and Bijayá were of a religious turn of mind and always wishful to do something or other to please the gods. Once upon a time they resolved to worship Siva and Párvati, his wife, and to that end began to tend a bull, the favourite *váhan* or mount of the god. Now, it so happened that thieves lay in wait for the bull, and taking advantage of a moment of relaxed vigilance on the part of Kaûsik, seized upon and decamped with the animal. When soon afterwards, Kaûsik discovered his loss and thought of its probable consequences, his grief knew no bounds, and he went through thick and thin and swam across rivers to find a trace of the lost bull; but all in vain. Towards nightfall, as he was trudging wearily home, he met his sister, Bijayá, who had come to fetch water from the river.

"Brother, you are alone, where is your charge?" cried she astonished.

Kaûsik answered by a flood of tears. When at last, the fact was communicated to her, she bade him have patience and said that they should not return home but go together in search of the bull all that night. So they set out.

They made their way into the depths of a neighbouring forest that seemed to get denser the further they went and there saw, with bated breath, bright beings, brighter than the moon that shone on them, seated upon a large plot of green and performing a *pujáh* to a certain deity. They were celestial beings and were conscious of the presence of Kaûsik and his sister. So, one of them arose and accosted them saying, "Who are you and what are you here for, ye children of men?" Trembling they said that they had come there in search of a bull they had lost. The angels knew what it meant, for the theft of the bull had been a mere ruse to test the sincerity of the worshippers' hearts. So their spokesman said again,

"You will have your missing bull back when you have performed the Budháshtami ceremony you have found us engaged in. Go home and obey, and when you have finished, the bull will return of his own accord."

They retraced their steps home; and when they had rested themselves and all the necessary offerings had been got together, they performed the ceremony—a labour of love. The goddess worshipped is none other than Párvati herself. She was highly pleased, and, presently, appeared before the startled gaze of the youthful devotees leading the missing bull and smiling as only a propitiated goddess can smile. She also expressed a wish that Kaûsik and Bijayá should each ask for a boon. Kaûsik said,

"Mother, if you will make your servant happy, grant that I may be a king."

And Bijayá said, "Mother, I pray to be wife to such a bright being as I have seen on the green-sward in the forest."

The goddess said, "It shall be as you both wish."

A few days later, the king of Pátaliputra died, and the ministers met in council to deliberate on the state of affairs. The king had left no children to succeed him; but for all that, the throne could not be allowed to remain unoccupied. They, therefore, decided upon seeking for a king to mount it, and whom but Kaûsik should they pitch upon? When he was brought before them in a perfect ecstasy of joy, the grey-headed officers of state discovered a *raj-tiká* [1] on his forehead and the signs of a *chakravartee* [2] on the palms of his hands and the soles of his feet. And they exclaimed,

"Here we have found a king born to rule over men! Let us go and proclaim him to the people by the beat

[1] A mark of royalty. [2] Suzerain.

of tom-toms, and let them rejoice and cry victory to Mahárájá Kaûsik!"

Thus Kaûsik became a king, and the promise made to him by Párvati was fulfilled.

And when Kaûsik became a king, Bijayá became a princess. She was young and beautiful as a lily in full bloom. For her hand flocked to Kaûsik's court kings and princes from all parts of the earth. So there was convened a big assembly of kings and princes, and all the world crowded to see whom Bijayá might select as her husband. When she was led into the assembly by Kaûsik, robed in gorgeous attire, and holding the customary garland of white flowers and vessel of curd—the one to throw round the neck of the happy youth of her choice and the other as an auspicious present to him—her eyes and, with them, her soul were riveted upon a young prince of extraordinary comeliness. Just then a voice came through the air, loud enough to be heard by all present:

"Choose him, Bijayá, and fulfil your destiny."

And Bijayá put her garland of white flowers round his neck and was led away by him. The bridegroom was none other than Yama, the king of the dead.

Bijayá was taken home to Yama-*puri*, the residence of her lord, Yama, and was told by him that she might go where she listed provided she took care not to visit the southern portion of the grounds around the house. Bijayá delighted in her daily walks amidst the trees and flowers, and for some time she dutifully avoided the south, but one day her curiosity overcame her dutiful obedience, and she found herself on the forbidden ground. Now, it is in the south that the places of torment for women who have sinned in life are situate, and she witnessed a horrible scene. Thousands of women of all ages and conditions were writhing and twisting in raging fires that burnt them to the marrow yet killed them not, and their piteous cries rent the air. But what horrified Bijayá most of all was to see her own mother among the sufferers. "Bijayá, my own flesh and blood," cried she from the blazing furnace, "save me, O, save your mother!"

Bijayá weeping said, "What has brought you here, mother, what sins did you commit?"

"Alas!" replied the poor woman, "I refused to feed a Bráhman who was hungry and I robbed another of his substance. But surely, I have had enough punishment; have pity on me now!"

Bijayá promised her speedy deliverance and returned to her palace in a state of mind that can be better imagined than described. When she next saw Yama, she threw herself at his feet, sobbing and choking in grief. Yama cried in astonishment, "What is the matter with you, wife?" She unbosomed herself, telling him the whole story and concluded with, "It behoves you, my husband, to look to her case, my lord. Consider she is your wife's own mother." Then Yama replied,

"I could not help her even though she were my own, pretty one. People reap as they sow; Vidhátá (God) himself cannot help them."

But it so happened that there was a remedy in this particular case and Yama after deep thought told his wife that if she could induce her brother, Kaûsik, who enjoyed the reward given to those who had performed the Budháshtami ceremony to part with a portion of his reward in favour of his mother, the poor woman might purchase her freedom. Bijayá, with her husband's permission, forthwith set out on her mission confidently expecting success.

Ushered into the royal presence, the sister said to her brother,

"Brother, I have come on an important matter. Our mother, for sins committed in the flesh, is suffering in hell. She may, by favour of the king of the dead, be yet delivered from her dreadful misery, if you will part with a portion of the reward you have earned by the performance of the Budháshtami ceremonies and transfer it to her account."

And she described in heartrending terms how horribly their mother was being tortured, and how piteously she moaned and groaned. But Kaûsik, turning up the corners of his eyes and screwing down the corners of his mouth, said dryly, "I cannot allow myself to be poorer by one pice worth of the merit that has gained me a throne."

Bijayá was cruelly disappointed, and she returned home to tell Yama what an ungrateful, stone-hearted, graceless wretch her brother, Kaûsik, had become. Then Yama said,

"Such are the ways of men. But once again, Bijayá, go down to the earth and see if any other person be more agreeable to your wishes. In the country of Banga is a poor Bráhman woman whose name is Gaûtami. She is at present suffering extreme tortures in child-birth. She also is entitled to the bliss arising from the performance of the Budháshtami ceremony. Try if she will barter a portion of the reward that is her due in return for immunity from her throes. Bijayá, disguise yourself as a shepherdess, hasten to Banga and see the woman without delay."

So, dressed like a shepherdess, Bijayá presented herself to Gaûtami whom she found on the point of death with agony. She made her proposal, whereupon Gaûtami looked up and gasped out,

"No, shepherdess, I will not make such a disreputable bargain. My pain is for a while only, but Budháshtami has entitled me to eternal joy!"

"You know not what you say, mother," argued Bijayá, "life is all and everything. If you live, you may perform many a Budháshtami ceremony more. But if you let yourself die when the remedy is within your reach, you kill yourself and thus deserve hell. Reject not my offer."

Then Gaûtami pondered well and at last agreed to grant Bijayá's prayer, whereupon Bijayá returned home rejoicing. Her mother was, by reason of Gaûtami's sacrifice, delivered from torment and translated direct to heaven. The manifold blessings of a performance of the Budháshtami ceremony were proclaimed throughout the earth, and it was and still is observed everywhere.

So, ye all that have listened to this sacred *kathá*, cry victory to Párvati;—*ulu! ulu! ulu!*

V.

THE MANGAL-CHANDI CEREMONY.

[This goddess, who is merely a transformation of the dread *Káli*, has been described in the *Kálikápurán* as a very beautiful and youthful being of fair complexion, seated on a red lotus, and having a crown of light on her head. She is dressed in red and is worshipped in images of clay or stone, but more usually a small earthen pitcher is used; this she is supposed to fill with her presence when invoked with the proper *mantras*.[1] She is sometimes represented by a few blades of grass and nine grains of *Áman* or winter rice enclosed in a piece of plantain leaf folded in the form of an equilateral triangle.]

THE TALE.

The Goddess who Devoured Elephants.

RATNÁKAR SÁDHU was a rich merchant and had two wives, Lahaná and Khullaná. Lahaná, being the younger, was the better beloved and, naturally enough, looked upon with no loving eye by her rival, the elder wife. Lahaná always spoke ill of her to her husband and at last succeeded so far with him as to have the object of her jealousy banished from her home.

After many wanderings and hardships it came about that poor Khullaná was forced to earn a scanty living by tending a flock of goats in a far-off country. She

[1] Formulae of invocation, worship, etc.

was always sad and her only thoughts were of her husband and the home she had been forced to leave behind her. One day, whilst brooding over her hard lot, her ears caught the sound of cymbals and conch-shells in a village hard by. Curiosity led her to the spot, for she wanted to see what *pujáh* it was that the people were performing. She questioned them, and was told it was the goddess Mangal-Chandi (the *auspicious* Chandi) whom they were worshipping. "What is this *pujáh* for?" cried she, "What can the goddess do for her worshippers?"

"Anything and everything," replied they, "if you are poor and want wealth, if you are barren and long for a child, if you are down in your luck and seek after happiness, you shall have your wish, provided you worship Mangal-Chandi in due form and in sincerity of heart. If you doubt what we say let us tell you the story of what happened to a huntsman and you will be convinced. Here it is:

Now the story goes that there was once a poor follower of the chase who fed his family on what he earned by his bow and arrows. It so happened that on one occasion he roamed through the length and breadth of the forest, but did not see trace of even so poor an animal as a hare. All the beasts had (as he afterwards learned) taken refuge with the goddess Mangal-Chandi and had implored her protection from their would-be destroyers. The goddess, accordingly, determined to present herself in person to the huntsman who was just returning home at high noon with a very rueful face. She appeared before his dazzled gaze in a halo of heavenly effulgence illumining the forest around her and surcharging the air with a divine perfume.

And before the hunter of wild animals had recovered from his surprise, she accosted him saying,

"Huntsman, here is an ingot of gold, only an earnest of many more that you will ere long be presented with on condition that you throw down your weapons and pursue your cruel trade no more."

The man threw his bow and quiver down and prostrated himself at the feet of his august visitor, and when he rose, the goddess had disappeared. He betook himself home with the speed of one of the stags of the wood and in a trice acquainted his wife by word, gesture, and action with what good fortune had befallen them. The couple locked in each other's arms entered their hut together where in a corner—O joy and madness!—they discovered a thousand more ingots of gold. The hut was in a short time replaced by a splendid building; and servants, horses, elephants, and all the appurtenances of wealth soon made the lucky pair equal to the proudest in the land.

But this sudden affluence attracted the notice of the king of the country, who sent an army to the house of the huntsman with instructions to bring him bound hand and foot together with all his wealth to the palace. These orders were obeyed to the letter, and you can conceive how great the distress of the poor huntsman was! He fell prostrate on the floor of the prison-cell assigned to him and in an ecstasy of grief prayed Mangal-Chandi to help him. She was not slow to listen to his prayers, and quickly appeared again in her divine splendour and assured him of her protection. "For," said she, "it was I who made you great, and I it is who shall save you from ruin." At night, therefore, she appeared before the king in a dream and rated him soundly for handling the unoffending huntsman so roughly :

"Do you hold your life, and the lives of all of your house even to the last scion, and your kingdom, and all that belongs to it to be worth even so much as a grain of sand ? If you do, hasten with all speed to release the huntsman, return him his gold, and as a compensation for the trouble you have given him, console him with the hand of the princess, your daughter, and half of your kingdom into the bargain. This," continued the wrathful goddess, "you shall do to-morrow and not later. You should have known that he is a worshipper of mine and, as such, under my protection."

The poor, terrified king got up with a shudder and ran to where the huntsman had been kept in prison. He struck off his fetters with his own hands, humbled himself to the dust before his former prisoner, and conducted him with royal honours to the palace. There he availed himself of the earliest auspicious hour to unite the princess and the favoured of the deity in the holy bonds of matrimony.

The story, thus told, filled Khullaná more than ever with a desire to worship the goddess. But she was so poor that she had not wherewith to perform the *pujáh*. She had but nine grains of rice, a flower, and a few blades of grass. Yet she resolved to carry out the ceremony with these for want of better offerings. This she soon did, and no sooner had she opened her eyes after an interval of calm meditation than she saw her husband before her looking so penitent and asking her with many expressions of love to return home with him. Needless to say that she consented, and thereafter lived as happily as any wife might wish to do.

Years rolled on. Khullaná gave birth to a son who was named Sadánand and who grew up a charming lad, the joy of his mother's heart. But his father was not there to share her joy, for it so happened that ere Sadánand first saw the light, Ratnákar had set out on a trading expedition to Sinhal (Ceylon) and had never returned. When the boy was old enough to learn, he was sent to the village school. There he made friends, as every boy does, and they used all to sit together and chat in the intervals of lessons.

One day they began to talk about their fathers, but Sadánand kept silent, for he had never known his, not even his name. Some of his ill-natured companions taunted him with being base-born, and as one whose father was, nobody knew who. Sadánand, pained at heart, came home, and shut himself up in his room filled with sorrow. His mother soon knocked at the door anxious to learn the cause of his grief. Admitted after a great deal of knocking, she hugged him to her bosom, kissed him over and over again, and fondled him ; but for a long time he would not speak a word. At length,

"Mother," said he, "I have been shamed this day by my school-fellows. I could not tell them who my father is or what his name, and they called me nobody's child. Tell me who my father was, what was his name, and whether he is living or dead. If not, I stop in this room, nor will I taste of food until death puts an end to my misery." Khullaná wept, for grief weighed heavy upon her heart to be thus reminded of her husband who had not been heard of for many a long year. But she wiped her tears away to console her child with the assurance that he was the son of as good a father as could be wished for and referred him to her maid for his name (for wives do not utter the names of their husbands), and also told him—she could scarcely speak for tears—that he had gone to trade in Sinhal and since then had not been heard of. The lad heard his mother in silence and for a long time did not speak a word; he was evidently deep in thought.

"Mother, where is this Sinhal and how far?" cried he, at last breaking silence.

"A long way off, dear, a very long way off," replied she, "further than I can tell."

"But I will go there, mother, in search of father; you will not prevent me?"

"Will you?" cried the mother in bewilderment, "you—go to Sinhal—impossible! It cannot be while I live." She clasped Sadánand to her bosom, filled with terror at the idea of losing him. But he was a headstrong boy used to having his own way, so after a weary interchange of ayes and noes and coaxing, threatening, and weeping on one side and a display of obstinacy on the other, it was settled that Sadánand should go in search of his father as soon as Mangal-Chandi had been worshipped with due ceremony. The *pujáh*, accordingly, was duly performed on the first auspicious day, and Sadánand straightway set sail in a fleet of seven vessels filled with merchandise.

But now let us turn back for a while and see how matters had fared with Ratnákar Sádhu and why it was that he had not been heard of for such a time. After leaving home he had a prosperous voyage and reached the territory of the king of Sinhal long before he expected to. At some distance from the capital a very strange sight met his eyes. He there saw in front of him a floating forest of lotuses in a small river that surrounded the city; and there of a morning, in the bright light of the rising sun, there appeared the image of a young woman of transcendent beauty seated upon a large flower and holding a big elephant in each hand which she devoured and threw off alternately. The Sádhu wishing to make capital out of what he had seen hastened to the king as soon as he landed at the *ghat* of the palace, and told him of this strange phenomenon.

At first the king absolutely refused to believe his story, but on the merchant swearing to the truth of what he had averred and inviting him to come and see it for himself, it was settled that the king, attended by his court, should go down to the river side, but before doing so he threatened the audacious foreigner with severe punishment if his statement should prove false. And false it proved, for when the king and his court came to the spot indicated, nothing was to be seen—no maiden of transcendent beauty seated on a lotus holding a big elephant in each hand which she was devouring and throwing off alternately—not even the floating forest of lotuses itself. Flying into a rage, the king stripped the unfortunate Sádhu of all that he had, both on his person and in his fleet, and threw him into a prison there to atone for his monstrous lie.

The story of Sadánand's voyage to Sinhal was his father's re-told. He too found the winds and tides favourable until they brought him to where his father's misfortune had begun, and he too saw the miracle.

Of course, he went to the king and told him of what he had witnessed. But in his case the king pursued

'A young woman of transcendent beauty seated upon a large flower and holding a big elephant in each hand.'

Face page 54

a different course. The very mention of the phenomenon threw him into a rage and the fiat went forth to his executioner—"Go, load the Sádhu with fetters and cut him to pieces."

Sadánand in his distress besought the intercession—not of any mortal man but—of his tutelary goddess, Mangal Chandi, whom his mother had taught him to love and adore. And the goddess in her mercy worked a miracle. The king was by some unseen agency induced to go to the *ghat* and from thence, as sure as the sun was in the sky, he saw with his eyes the maiden of transcendent beauty seated upon a lotus holding in each hand a big elephant which she was alternately devouring and throwing off.

This was followed by a waking dream in which the goddess, Mangal Chandi, appeared to him in person and bade him do no harm to Sadánand and his father.

"For," said the deity, "they are my worshippers and beloved of me. If aught of further evil befall them through you, I shall spare neither you, nor your race, nor your kingdom, nor anything pertaining to you. Go and release them both; and give them what you have taken from them, and half your kingdom, and your daughter in marriage to Sadánand, my favourite."

The goddess vanished. It took the king but a few minutes to start to his feet, to compose himself, to run to the state-prison, to release the father and son, and to throw himself at their feet crying, "O, take all that I have, but save me and my race!"

What followed can easily be guessed. The father and son met for the first time in their lives and their joy was indescribable, their merchandise was restored to them, and the good king gave Sadánand his charming daughter in marriage and half the kingdom for a dowry. What mortal could have pictured such a happy ending to their sorrows.

And then came the voyage homeward bound. Wind and weather were both favourable, and in far less time than they had counted on, they had their fleet moored at the *ghat* at home. Khullaná was then worshipping Mangal Chandi; and just as she was going to eat a mouthful devoutly and dutifully from the consecrated dish, some one near by cried out, "Khullaná, Khullaná, Ratnákar Sádhu and Sadánand have returned." In a delirium of joy she thoughtlessly threw down the mouthful on the ground and hurried off to the *ghat*, but, alas, only to see the fleet with Ratnákar and Sadánand on board sink beneath the waves. Casting about in her mind as to how she might have transgressed, she remembered how she had thrown down the sacred food and had thus insulted the deity.

Khullaná was quick to recognise that in some way she had given offence to the goddess and that this was her punishment.

Filled with remorse she ran home, picked up the food, placed it upon her head and her heart, and ate it. Then she again hastened with all speed to the river-bank, and this time was rewarded by finding the fleet riding at anchor with Ratnákar and Sadánand on board, safe and well.

The misfortunes of the family were now at an end. Khullaná took her husband and her son with his newly married wife home with all due ceremonies and observances; and by the ever-continuing favour of Mangal Chandi, they lived happily together for many long years.

So ye all that have listened to this sacred *kathá*, cry victory to Mangal Chandi;—*ulu! ulu! ulu!*

VI.

THE JANMASHTAMI CEREMONY.

[This Ceremony is performed on the anniversary of the nativity of *Krishna*, an *avatár* or incarnation of Vishnu. Images in stone or metal of this deity are to be found in the houses of many Hindus. He is generally represented by a *Sálagrám Silá* —a round piece of black, calcareous stone.]

THE TALE.

The Slayer of Kangsa.

WHERE Vishnu, the great Preserver of creation, lay in his eternal bed on the crest of the great Serpent, Ananta, in the ocean of milk, thither proceeded Bramhá the Creator, Shiva the Destroyer, and all the lesser gods of heaven at the instance of Basundhará, the earth. Let me tell you why. Basundhará had of late suffered much at the hands of Kangsa, king of Mathurá, who had developed into a harsh tyrant and oppressor of men. So, she had come to heaven and lodged her complaint with Shiva—the most accessible of the divine three—who had taken her to Bramhá, and at his advice, had called a meeting of the princes of heaven. And so it came about that the gods had assembled in order to lay the petition of Basundhará before Vishnu and advocate her cause. When they reached the shore, they raised their hands and their voices in praise of their over-lord, and mounted each upon a drake, glided through the waves to where he lay, singing :—

"Thou that hast the complexion of the *Atasi* flower
And eyes like the petals of a lotus,
That art charming as an autumnal moon,
Art clothed in yellow and garlanded with flowers,
Favour us.
Thou hast the *Kaûstav*[1] at thy navel and jewels all over thy person,
That art infinite in virtues, the receptacle of the universe,
Art seed of creation and eternal,
We bow to thee—favour us."

And the god of heaven shaking off his slumbers looked at the assembled psalm-singers and said, "Gods, why are ye here ?" They told him their reason and pleaded eloquently for Basundhará. Then to them Vishnu made answer,

"Her case is hard, indeed. I it was who made Kangsa great; great indeed is he, but his might is in my might; but abused, as I hear, his power has been, worse shall yet befall him and he shall bite the dust. I remember well I granted him a prayer, when he had pleased me with his *pujáhs*, that none but his sister's son should kill him. Let Basundhará, however, take heart, for I shall myself arise as his nephew—be born of Devaki, his sister, in the city of Mathurá—and kill the tyrant. This I will do; but let Shiva, my colleague, lend me the helping hand of his spouse, Párvati. She shall have to be born simultaneously with me of Yasodá in Braja."

With this Vishnu dismissed the gods, who rode away rejoicing.

In the month of Bhádra (September), on the eighth night after the full moon, of Devaki, the sister of Kangsa,

[1] A gem.

was born a son; the reader already knows who he was. And at the same time, of Yasodá, a milkman's wife, was born a daughter; needless to say, she was Párvati herself. Now Kangsa, the tyrant, had been killing the children of Devaki—as many as she had brought forth—for he knew it was by the hand of one of them he should fall, and he had thought by this means to avert his fate. Devaki's boundless joy at having a son born to her was soon turned to grief and despair when she remembered that he had but one short night to live, for on the following morn the myrmidons of the cruel Kangsa would come and destroy him. Filled with these bitter thoughts she was aroused by a voice saying:—

"Do thou, Devaki, exchange thy son for the new-born daughter of Yasodá, a milk-woman of Braja."

In obedience to the command Devaki handed over her baby with many a kiss and tear which it seemed to understand perfectly to her husband, Vasudeva, who started off with the precious charge in his arms.

On his way he had to cross the Jumná. Who would be there to ferry him over at dead of night? But it must not be forgotten that the child was Vishnu himself and in that sore emergency he worked a miracle. Standing on the edge of the broad and deep river, as Vasudeva was looking about for a boat or raft, he saw a jackal wading across the water; and though he much marvelled at the circumstance, yet he followed in its track and so got safely to the other side. Then he noticed that although it was raining heavily all around yet no moisture reached him or the child. Filled with wonder at this he at last looked up when to his astonishment he perceived something resembling the hood of an enormous snake sheltering him and the child from the downpour. The great serpent, Ananta, himself was there. Vasudeva's heart was filled with awe, but he sped on.

Yasodá was asleep with her new-born daughter, and without waking her Vasudeva exchanged the children. His purpose achieved, he returned to Mathurá with Yasodá's baby in his arms. At daybreak Kangsa's men were at the door to take away Devaki's child, and she had no choice but to deliver it to the executioners. Surprised though he was to find that the infant was a girl and not a boy Kangsa, nevertheless, ordered it to be dashed against a stone that lay hard by. One of his men at once seized the child and raising it aloft was on the point of dashing it down, when, to the amazement of all present, it escaped from his grasp and ascended to heaven. Kangsa, amazed and bewildered, raised his eyes when he saw, seated upon her lion, Párvati herself bedimming with her lustre the bright god of day. With a glance that pierced the king through and through she looked at him and then in stern tones uttered words of prophecy, "He that is to kill you shall grow up in Braja!"

All happened as had been predicted. The so-called son of Yasodá grew to manhood and when the time ordained by the gods arrived he fulfilled his mission by killing Kangsa—the tyrant of whom Basundhará had become sick. The circumstances were most romantic. Kangsa had made many attempts to slay the child in his infancy, but all of them had signally failed. The mightiest of Asuras (giants) whom he had despatched for the purpose had been themselves slain by Vishnu. At last, he invited Vishnu with the other denizens of Braja to a great sacrifice. Vishnu came, broke Kangsa's great bow, slew the infuriated elephant Kangsa had treacherously stationed at his gate to attack him and his elder brother, Balarám, disposed of some gigantic wrestlers whom the king had appointed to wrestle with him, and at last sprang upon Kangsa himself as he sat on his throne and dragging him down slew him. It goes without saying that Kangsa went to heaven, his salvation being effected by his constantly thinking of Vishnu who was to slay him.

So, ye all that have listened to his sacred *kathá*, cry victory to Vishnu ;—*ulu ! ulu ! ulu !*

VII.

THE PADMA PUJAH CEREMONY.

[Padmá is Manasá under another name, but as Padmá she is worshipped with greater pomp and ceremony. Goats and buffaloes are sometimes sacrificed to her. She is regarded by sailors as their patroness; and many of them do not fail to celebrate her *pujáh* before starting on a long and perilous voyage. They often call themselves *Padmá-putras* or sons of Padmá. People worship Padmá to save their tenements from destruction by the encroachment of rivers as well as to conciliate the favour of her children, the snakes. The goddess is represented as having four hands. The *kathá* as narrated in the following pages is a *résumé* of the Padmá-Purána—the Padmá-worshippers' Bible.]

THE TALE.

Chánd, the Unbeliever.

ONCE upon a time Mahádeo, the great god of heaven, visited the earth in human form. In the course of his wanderings he met a young woman of the abominable *kotch* caste, but her surpassing charms made up for the lowness of her birth; at least, the god took no exception to it. He was fired with an intense desire which was reciprocated by the woman. Their acquaintance ripened and in the course of time a female child was born to them, but, wonder of wonders, the girl was full-grown from her birth. However, nothing is impossible where a god is concerned. The mother of the girl—she called the child Padmá—was filled with consternation and fled leaving her daughter to the tender mercies of an unknown fate. Padmá, however, being a goddess born, was not destined to suffer for want of protection and followed Maháde o to heaven.

Now, it so happened that Bhagavati, the wedded wife of Mahádeo, was standing at the door of her house to welcome her knight-errant home, and when she saw him coming with the beautiful Padmá accompanying him her heart was torn with jealousy, for of a truth the gods and goddesses enjoy no immunity from those passions that beset the heart of man. Rushing forward Bhagavati seized the unoffending girl, and without the least pity tore out one of her eyes with her nails. Mahádeo, however, managed to elude the clutches of the furious goddess and taking up his position at a respectful distance, remonstrated :

"It is no rival of yours but my daughter, Padmá. Remove all suspicion from your mind,—it becomes you not."

He then began to shed tears on seeing the sorry plight Padmá was in. Now, nothing that emanates from a god's body is worthless ; the tears assumed a definite shape ; and lo ! a girl of exquisite beauty stood before the god whom the dwellers of heaven agreed to call Netá, inasmuch as she was born of *Netra-bári* which means tears. Mahádeo was consoled, for he had now found a companion for Padmá, and he dismissed them both with his blessings.

The two girls wandered through heaven homeless and owned by none. Soon, however, they made the acquaintance of, and in a short time became hand-

and-glove with, an *Apsara* couple, musicians, who performed at the court of Indra, the king of Amarávati, and at their advice came down to the earth and fixed their abode there. Here Netá commenced the business of a laundress out of sheer necessity, but the clothes she washed belonged to the deities.

Now, it so happened that in the particular region where Padmá and Netá settled, there lived Chánd Saodágar, a man equal in wealth to a million of millionaires and in influence, the greatest of all men. Padmá was only half a goddess, for with her divine blood was mingled the human. Nevertheless, she greatly coveted the *pujáh* that man offered to goddesses. She longed to be established in the pantheon to which, she thought, she had as good a right as any female deity. And she knew it would not be hard to get her wish if only Chánd Saodágar pleased to take the initiative; for, then, all the rest of mankind would follow his example.

But Chánd was an obdurate old gorilla, who would not accept Padmá for a deity and would not worship her, though she pleaded hard and with tears that she was the child of Mahádeo and had as much of his blood in her veins as his sons Kártika and Ganesha. Supplication, coaxing, and threats failing, her blood rose, she vowed revenge—for was she not, after all, the daughter of Mahádeo, the Destroyer—and uttering threats and curses departed.

Now, Padmá had married Jaratkáru; and by him was mother of an innumerable progeny of snakes of all sorts and sizes. These she now let loose upon the six sons of Chánd who were one by one bitten to death before the eyes of their old and loving father. As each one lost his life Padmá appeared to Chánd and said,

"Saodágar, this is not by chance or in the course of nature. Even now, before it is too late, yield and worship me!"

But the old man had a stubborn heart and preferred to lose all his remaining sons rather than fall into the grievous error of worshipping an impostor. And equally resolved was Padmá to have what she considered was her birthright.

Chánd Saodágar could not now bear to live in the house where he had lost his dear sons, and though his wife was in ill-health he fitted out a large fleet and sailed away for a distant country. But Padmá was at his heels; and when he had reached a certain lake called Kálidaha, she determined to sink his vessels. As, however, the water in the lake was not deep enough to completely cover the ships, she borrowed more from the seven oceans of the earth and then to accomplish her object raised a furious storm through the agency of Pavana, the god of the winds. But here an unexpected difficulty rose up in her path and seemed likely to defeat her object. Chánd was a devout worshipper of Bhagavati, the step-mother of Padmá, and when the storm was raging, he prayed to the goddess with great earnestness to come down and save him. And the goddess came and sat on the prow of Chánd's vessel. As long as she did so it skimmed lightly upon the water and would not sink. At this emergency, Padmá besought the aid of her father:

"Father, see how my step-mother crosses me at every turn. Is she not content with blinding one of my eyes and banishing me from heaven, without seeking to defeat all my purposes?"

And Mahádeo felt for her and descending from Kâilás,

his abode, appeared before his high-mettled consort with the purpose of making her, if possible, quit the vessel. He began as follows:

"By the heads of your favourite sons, Kártika and Ganesha, you must leave the vessel and come away directly, O Bhagavati, or—"

"Or, what?" flashed out his spouse.

"Nothing," replied Mahádeo in a lower key, "I do not mean anything. But, Bhagavati, my darling, you should not press your point in all matters. Is it not bare justice to poor Padmá that she should have her way once? Remember, she has been cruelly wronged. You were wont to be generous."

And Bhagavati yielded, and arm-in-arm with her husband re-ascended to heaven leaving Chánd to his fate. The next blast upset his vessel, and he was forced to swim for his life. At this Padmá appeared in the air above Chánd's head and said:

"Saodágar, do you not realise that this is not by chance or in the course of nature. Even now yield and worship me whilst there is yet time!"

But he still refused even though he was drowning. Padmá, however, did not mean to kill him. So, after drifting in the water for some days, he was at length allowed to reach the shore but not before he had been made the subject of many illusions by Padmá, in which he thought himself to be continually in sight of land only to find nothing but water as far as the eye could reach. At each fresh disappointment Padmá reiterated her appeals but in vain.

The Saodágar was allowed to reach the shore after all, as I have said, but by that time he was dying with hunger and exhaustion. Looking around, he thought he saw some delicious fruits lying on the sand. He got up as best he could and stretched his hand forward to reach them. But lo! when nearly in his grasp they vanished and at the same time the ground began to sink under his feet, and he was like to be in water again. Just then his tormentress again appeared in the air and asked him to yield, but all to no effect.

The *Apsara* couple who were Padmá's friends were in sympathy with her wishes, and formed a plan to help her. It was this: that one of them should subject himself to re-birth as Chánd's son and that the other should be born as the daughter of a Saodágar of Ujáninagar, Sáha Beniah by name; that they should both grow up and be united in marriage, and thus one being the only son of Chánd whilst the other would be his dear daughter-in-law, they would secure very great influence over him which could be used for the sole purpose of bringing him round to the worship of Padmá. Accordingly, five or six months after Chánd had set sail from home, to him was born a son who was named Lakhindar; and to Sáha was born some time later a daughter to whom the poetical name of Behulá was given. It is needless to say that Lakhindar was to Chánd, who after many further trials and privations had at last reached home, "dearer than eye-sight, space, and liberty."

Now when Lakhindar came of age, he chose Behulá to be his wife, and they arranged to be married. It must be borne in mind that the *Apsara* couple, in their present re-birth as Lakhindar and Behulá, retained no consciousness of their former state; and it was only by virtue of their divinity, that they felt a strong desire to serve and glorify Padmá—the mission which they had set themselves.

Just as preparations for the wedding were being made, Chánd was startled after many a year of comfortable oblivion by the too well-known form and voice of Padmá:

"Saodágar," said she, "I have not given up my resolve but have only been waiting my opportunity. Your son, Lakhindar, is going to marry to-night. The occasion is a joyous one. You seem to have forgotten your past misfortunes; you are happy and look hopefully to the future. But I have it in my power to turn your happiness into the deepest woe in a minute and this I will do, unless you yield and worship me before the bride and bridegroom are united."

Chánd shuddered to think what might happen, but yet he did not yield, although Lakhindar himself besought him with tears to do so.

Chánd knew full well that Padmá would wreak her vengeance upon him by having his only son, Lakhindar, bitten to death by her snakes, it might be, on the very night of the wedding. So, he had an iron house constructed in which Lakhindar was to live with his lovely bride, and into which there was no aperture for any thing but air to enter. The nuptials were duly solemnised, and the married couple retired into their iron house. Padmá's time had come, and rousing her sons she sent them out on the fell mission of biting Lakhindar to death. They came and went round and round the house but could not enter it. Towards the close of the night they returned to their mother after a last fruitless endeavour to effect an entrance, and were severely rebuked by Padmá for their failure. The first night passed away and Lakhindar was still unharmed. On the following day Padmá chose the cleverest of her sons, Kálkut by name, for the difficult task. Now Kálkut had the gift of squeezing himself into the smallest size and expanding himself at his will. At dead of night he entered the iron house through a hole no bigger than the circumference of a needle, and though he felt very reluctant to kill one who looked so charming and divine in his peaceful sleep, yet he could not choose but bite him. Lakhindar died instantly; and Behulá awoke to pierce the night air with her loud wailings.

Chánd's heart was about to break; his determination was shaken. And when Behulá pleaded,

"O, yield, father-in-law, yield, and worship Padmá, and let my Lakhindar be restored to me and let me live." He replied, "I shall, but let my son be first brought to life."

Behulá had a wooden raft made, and taking her dead husband upon it she launched alone upon a voyage in quest of Padmá. From one country to another she went inquiring of man, of beast, and of the fowl of the air—of all she met on her weary way—if they knew Padmá and where she lived. They all said, "We know her not, nor where she lives."

Meanwhile, Mahádeo and Bhagavati happened to be taking a trip through the sky, and the goddess who, looking down, had descried Behulá on her raft called her husband's attention to her and her mournful charge. "Lord of the ghosts, who and what is she, and what is she about?" she inquired.

They descended together and hovered over the raft. Behulá told them her sad story and made her oft-repeated inquiry: "Do you know Padmá and where she lives?"

'Behulá . . . taking her dead husband . . . upon a voyage in quest of Padmá.'

Face page 70

Mahádeo could have raised a thousand and one Lakhindars from the dead if he had so willed, but he meant to reserve the feat for Padmá so that she might be glorified. Accordingly, he told Behulá the whereabouts of the goddess and the way to go there. The raft, by favour of the great god, shot over the weird waters with the speed of lightning and soon reached Padmá's abode. Padmá felt herself irresistibly drawn towards Behulá when they met, for they had been friends in a previous birth. And when Padmá was told that Chánd had consented to worship her on her bringing Lakhindar back to life, she readily performed the miracle that was asked of her and at the words, "Lakhindar, arise," Behulá's husband was restored to her.

Straightway the loving couple returned home rejoicing and filled Chánd and all his kingdom with raptures of joy. He now worshipped Padmá not merely to keep the promise he had made, but also out of a conviction of her might and out of gratitude for giving him back not only his Lakhindar, but also all his other long-lost sons and his sunken boats, for the propitiated goddess left none of her worshipper's losses unrepaired. And Chánd's example was soon followed by all the world, for he was a man of the greatest influence on earth, and every one felt bound to copy him.

Thus was the *pujáh* of Padmá celebrated here below, and she has ever since enjoyed her just rights among gods and men.

So, ye all that have listened to this sacred *kathá*, cry victory to Padmá;—*ulu! ulu! ulu!*

VIII.

THE SANKATA CEREMONY.

[Vishnu, the Preserver, one of the Hindu Triad, is worshipped under the appellation of Sankata-Náráyana every Tuesday in the fortnight of the full moon during the months from April to November. The reward that is expected is deliverance from perils of all sorts, existing or impending. The female worshipper has to go through the rites in a difficult posture—with her hands going beneath the knee-pit and folded in front of her face. The attitude is, perhaps, meant to be typical of dangers and difficulties. She has also to eat on the day of the *pujáh* in this attitude, her consecrated meal consisting of rice and six pieces of vegetable or fish—the latter, if she be not a widow.]

THE TALE.

The Gift of the Ascetic.

A CERTAIN king had three queens but not a single child by any of them. He was, therefore, in great depression of spirits, although he was in no want of abundance of this world's other goods. The people hated the childless chief, for childlessness signifies a sinful life in a previous existence, and looked upon him as a harbinger of evil. Even the man who swept the palace avoided seeing his face the first thing in the morning, lest the day should not pass well with him. One morning he roused his wife before day-break and said to her:

"Wife, get up and let me have my meal before I go to the palace. I see the childless king's face every morning and, as a consequence, do not get a full meal all the day. Let me have a hearty breakfast before I see that ill-omened countenance."

His breakfast over, the sweeper went to work. A woman of the palace noticed him chewing betel (as is the custom after a meal) and accosted him, saying,

"There, *Málee,* chewing betel? Have you broken your fast so early?"

"I have," returned the other; "I could not bear to go half empty every day from having seen the childless king's face the first thing in the morning."

Now, the king overheard this conversation, and the sweeper's answer was like gall and wormwood to him. He shut himself up in a room and would not see anybody nor do anything. But a holy *yogee* (ascetic) came to the door and insisted on being told of the grief of the king, on seeing him. The king was at last compelled to come out. The *yogee* said,

"You need not bewail your lot, my son, for you are, I see, destined to be a father, and that soon. Take this drug and let your queens eat of it, and they will not be long in becoming happy mothers. But promise me that one of the royal children shall be mine."

The king was too much delighted at this unexpected turn of fortune not to promise full compliance. And the holy man went his way.

The king handed over the drug to the eldest queen with instructions that it should be taken in equal portions by the three. But the eldest and the second were in league against the youngest; so they ate the gift up between themselves and threw away the cup from which they had eaten it. The youngest, however, got scent of the matter and running up and down the palace in an agony of rage and jealousy, happened to stumble upon the cup which she took up and fell to licking the inside of it with such energy that it shone again.

In due time the first and the second queens gave birth to two sons, but the third—lo! she gave birth to a conch-shell. The babes grew up to be very handsome lads and in the course of a few years made themselves familiar with all the learning of the age. Time flew; the princes were young men now, and the old king and his queens nearly forgot that they had been ushered into existence under a fearful contract with an ascetic that one of them should have to be made over to him whenever he should choose to come and put forward his claim.

But to return to the conch-shell. The queen kept it in her sleeping apartment, and could not find it in her heart to throw it away, although, apparently, it was nothing but a shell. She had not the remotest suspicion that it was anything but what it seemed, and you can judge of her surprise when one night—rather past the usual hour of sleep—looking by chance over her pillow, she perceived the conch-shell splitting in two and a young man of surpassing beauty issuing out of it! But she held her peace. When she woke again in the morning, the conch-shell was as it had always been, and no change in it could be seen. The strange sight was witnessed by the queen for three nights in succession, and she was now sure that it was not an illusion.

What do you think she did? Her heart was bursting

with joy at finding she had so fine a youth for her son. But as yet he was as none to her. She resolved to have him for herself at any risk. So, on the fourth night, as soon as the youth had again come out of his stronghold and gone on an errand of his own, the queen who was watching started up, seized the shell, and threw it into the fire, where it was consumed in a short time. Just then the young prince came in and seeing at a glance that his disguise was at an end, submitted to be presented to the world after some gentle expostulations to his mother. She strained him to her bosom, and both wept for joy.

Now it was that the ascetic came and a panic spread through the palace. Even though the king was able to induce himself to submit to the inevitable, the queens would not part with their sons for the world. A way was at last found out of the difficulty by substituting the son of a maid-servant. The ascetic took him, and the pair proceeded on their way until they came to a river which had to be crossed. The *yogee*, to test the young man, said,

"Well, prince, shall we send for the ferryman or swim across the water?"

"Let us swim across it," said the sham prince.

Next they came to a dense jungle, and the religious man proposed to call for some wood-cutters to cut a path through the forest or to make their way through it as best they could. The boy was for the latter. Now, all this proved that he was no king's son; for if he were, he, having been brought up in ease and luxury, would have called for a ferryman and wood-cutters rather than do the work himself. So they turned back and again came to the palace.

"You have deceived me, perjured king," cried the holy man in high indignation, "and my curse will not only consume your sons, but your whole race, and leave not one to bear your name!"

The trembling king had not a word to say, but brought forth the youngest prince—he that was born in a conch-shell—and the *yogee* was off again. The queen, the mother of the prince, was mad with grief and would not be consoled. But she had not had the courage to say nay to her lord. In the agony of her heart she threw herself on the ground before Sankata-Náráyan, the god of her household, and prayed to him with the utmost devotion. The god smiled upon her and appeared before her in a dream. He knew, omniscient that he was, what misfortune had been her way and what she would pray for. So addressing her,

"Daughter," said he, "cease weeping; for I bless your son and assure you that he will return to your bosom safe and unhurt in person; only continue to worship me and never waver in your faith!"

So saying, the god vanished.

Meanwhile the *yogee* and the prince had sped on and come to the same river and the same forest as the false prince had been brought to, and the same questions were put to the prince by his guide to test him. The prince would not cross the river but in a boat and would not traverse the forest but through a path cut by the woodmen. This was a prince, indeed!

At last he reached the abode of the ascetic, which was nothing better than a miserable hut in the midst of a wood. The *yogee* bade him help himself to what food there was and gave him permission to stroll about in any part of the wood except the south during his absence. Having given these instructions the ascetic set off to engage in one of his oft-recurring *yogs*—holy meditations—in a cremation *ghát* many a mile off. The prince bowed in acquiescence, and as soon as the holy man was gone, made good use of his permission to have a hearty meal of the fruits and roots which he found stowed away in a corner of the cottage and to sally out upon an expedition of discovery. He remembered the warning of his guardian that he should not go towards the south, but the more he thought about it the more curious and eager he grew to know what that forbidden quarter might be like. And so, after a few moments of hesitation he bent his steps towards the southern part of the wood; and scarcely had he gone a mile before a charming little building rose to view and around it a small garden of exquisite flowers. The prince lost no time in going up to it and knocking at the door, which was opened—wonder of wonders!—by a young damsel fairer than any of her sex whom he had ever seen or formed a conception of before. The girl blushed, and the prince stammered. Their confusion did not, however, last long, for shortly afterwards, the prince related his adventures, and the lady told him of things that were horrible to hear.

"The *yogee*, your guardian," said she, "is a *Tántrik*, that is to say, he propitiates his tutelary goddess, *Káli*, by horrible rites, one of which is the sacrifice of human beings at her altar. Hundreds have been slaughtered before to-day, and you and I will be the next victims unless we can contrive our escape or put an end to the monster before the dreadful day comes. The corpses of his victims are all yonder in a pond, and you may see them there."

The prince walked to the spot to have a look at the dead bodies ; and very great was his consternation when the severed heads laughed loud and long in his face and the trunks cut capers in the mud. He then returned to the maiden and sat long by her devising some means of escape.

Days and months passed away, and every day witnessed the prince and the maiden enjoying hours together in each other's company. Their perilous situation had lost its terror for them by long familiarity with it. But at last the day arrived on which the prince was to go the way of his predecessors. He was directed to bathe early and to fast, like persons who are to take part in a holy sacrificial ceremony. The *yogee*, telling him to keep at home till he returned, set off to light the sacrificial fire and perform the rites in due form in the burning *ghát* already mentioned. The prince, knowing what was in store for him, formed his plans in concert with the maiden, and awaited the issue with a brave heart.

In the evening the *Tántrik*, having finished the *pujáh*, came home to fetch the prince. While following his guide, the intended victim heard the roar of laughter that was proceeding from the pond, and arriving at the *ghát* he saw that the image of the goddess *Káli* had been set up in a shed and before her were heaps of flowers and *bel*-leaves ; he also saw the sacrificial lamps fed with *ghee*, the censer in which incense burnt in perfumed smoke, and the other requisites of a *pujáh*.

The prince paid his devotions to the goddess *standing* and prayed for strength. Scarcely had he finished when the *Tántrik* commanded him to prostrate himself before the altar. Thereupon he said,

"I am son of a king and do not know how to prostrate myself. Show me how to do it."

The *Tántrik* complying, laid himself flat upon his breast on the ground. And no sooner had he done so than the prince seized the sacrificial sword which was beside the altar and at one stroke severed his head from his body. Just at that instant the trunkless heads in the pond laughed more clamorously than ever, and the maiden of the forest presented herself before the joyful gaze of her lover. To run to the pond with some handfuls of flowers and *bel*-leaves from the altar and shower them upon the bodies in the mud was for them the work of a minute. And behold! the dead rose from their miry beds and blessed their deliverers in the fulness of their hearts.

That the prince and his fair companion were united in the sacred bonds of matrimony and that the mourning queen, his mother, the king, and the whole palace received the unexpected couple in transports of joy, goes without saying. And happily did Sankha-kumára—he who was born in a conch-shell—live with his charming bride, who too was a princess, through long, long years of love, peace, and prosperity. Thus was the benison of Sankata-Náráyan fulfilled, and devotion to his divinity proved fruitful of such good things as had never before been heard of.

So, ye all that have listened to this sacred *kathá*, cry victory to Sankata-Náráyan;—*ulu! ulu! ulu!*

IX.

THE KULA-MANGALBÁR CEREMONY.

[This *pujáh* is not very generally observed and does not obtain favour in all parts of Bengal. The peculiar features of the ceremony are that no images are made or contemplated; seventeen plums and the same number of plum-leaves are placed in a certain order upon a flat dish of copper dyed red with red-sandal paste, and these form the ostensible object of worship. The ceremony is performed on Tuesdays only.]

THE TALE.

The Sun's Twin Sons.

JOKÁI, of whom this story tells, was still young when her reputation for piety reached the ears of the king of the country in which she lived. She was of the high Bráhman caste and seems to have been unmarried, for no mention is made of her ever having a husband.

Now, the king we have spoken of had to perform the *Srádh* ceremony (obsequies) of his mother. For this purpose, amongst other things, a quantity of *áman* (*sun-dried*) rice was necessary. But it had been raining so hard for some time that though there was paddy in plenty, it could not be dried for want of the sun. The king, therefore, was in a sore strait and at his wit's end. Now, Jokái, by virtue of her great piety, had attained miraculous powers—so, at least, said her friends—it came about that in his perplexity he determined to send for her. In due course Jokái came—as in duty bound—and the king thus spake to her,

"Jokái, I require the sun, you must let me have him though only for a day, or I shall fall and my fathers shall fall, all through the non-accomplishment of the *Srádh.*"

It was, perhaps, a spirit of boastfulness that dictated Jokái's answer—sorely did she repent it afterwards. She said, "The sun shall be shining to-morrow at your palace, O King."

She was dismissed straightway with presents and promises of many more.

All the time intervening Jokái passed in worshipping the sun according to the *shástras*, and in praying to him, and in imploring his condescension with the greatest earnestness. But she felt that unless she offered him something more tempting than mere prayers, the god would turn a deaf ear to her solicitations. So, blushing at herself and trembling with an indefinite fear, she formally offered herself to the god and vowed that if he did her the favour of appearing on the following day, she should be his for evermore. The temptation was evidently too great for the god to resist, for next day he duly appeared and shone steadily and cheerfully throughout the day. Great was the fame of Jokái, and the king loaded her with gifts.

But Jokái was ill at ease. In the solitude of her lonely house she shuddered to think of the Sun. If the god came, what should she do then? She was ashamed of becoming a bride at her age. But the god *did* come. His day's work done, as soon as he had reached the Astáchal,[1] he drove direct to Jokái's house and knocked at the door :

"Jokái, my bride, I have come."

But Jokái hid herself in the darkest corner of the room and answered not. The god knocked away to his heart's content, but it was the door alone that responded by its rattling. Weary with waiting yet longing for Jokái, he at last decided to wed her in spirit, and this he did.

The poor woman finding herself a wife without an earthly husband, shut herself up in her house for shame and gave inquisitive people a wide berth. But people began to talk, and after an interval of some months the matter was brought to the notice of the king. He refused to believe the reports he had heard, but was yet induced to summon Jokái to court. She dressed herself in such a fashion as to deceive the eyes of the messengers ; and asking them to proceed by the public thoroughfare followed them through the forest by its side. On her way, unknown to the king's men, twin sons were born to her and these she left covered with dry leaves and went forward. At the palace she quickly proved herself to be but a victim of malicious slander ; and the king delighted at her purity dismissed her with presents.

On her return journey, passing through the forest, she took her deserted children and carried them home with her. Though the king was deceived, Jokái's neighbours had ears and at night they used to hear the wailing of children proceeding from her house. They told the king of the circumstance. Now, these children, who had been named Sukli and Akli, had the

[1] The mountain where the sun sets.

wonderful virtue of turning into a spoonful or so of blood in day-time as soon as exposed to the sun and of returning to their proper human shape at sunset. When, at the instigation of wicked people, the king sent messengers to Jokái's house to see if she had any children concealed there, the boys were about eight months old. The messengers arrived there at day-time when the children were in their liquid state; and Jokái forewarned of their approach poured them out at the foot of a plum-tree some distance from her house. The messengers found nothing and told the king so to his great pleasure.

Sukli and Akli henceforth made the plum-tree their abode and lived a predatory life upon whatever they could lay their hands on. Whoever passed under the tree with eatables in possession would be spoken to in a nasal tone, and the poor fellow, not knowing where the voice came from, would run for dear life from the supposed ghosts, dropping everything on the ground as he went. The food instantly passed into the ownership of the children of the Sun to their very great glee.

Once upon a time, a merchant vessel, brimful of rich cargo, was passing along the river hard by when Sukli and Akli shouted out from their tree "What have you got there in your vessel?" Some of the crew answered haughtily, "Nothing." And instantly, behold! there was nothing, indeed, in the boat. The merchant was overwhelmed with grief. He had, however, wit enough to jump ashore and run to where the tree stood. Failing to find anybody beneath or upon it, he addressed the tree itself:

"O Tree, O mighty Tree, I have sinned against you

by telling you an untruth in a contumacious spirit —forgive me."

Sukli answered, "We are twin brothers here, sons of the Sun. Worship us and preach the *pujáh* to the inmates of the earth ; it shall be well for you and them. Worship us with seventeen plums, and the same number of plum-leaves, and blades of the holy grass, and rice, and other offerings acceptable to the gods."

And when the merchant had performed the *pujáh*, following the directions received in every particular, and the twin brothers had been satisfied, Akli said, speaking to the merchant,

"Go now, saodágar, and be happy ; for as soon as you shall stand on the bank of the river and say,

'Akli-Sukli laugh in glee,
Treasures mine, come back to me,'

your merchandise shall be restored to you and be even as it was."

It happened as had been predicted and the merchant went home rejoicing and preached the new *pujáh* throughout the world under the name of the *Kul-mangalbár* ceremony.

So, ye all that have listened to this sacred *kathá*, cry victory to Akli-Sukli ;—*ulu ! ulu ! ulu !*

X.

THE DÁN-SANKRÁNTI CEREMONY.

[The time for this ceremony is during the last days of *Chait* and *Baisákh* corresponding to April and May of the English calendar. The reward is beatitude after death. The whole ceremony and its *kathá* point to the moral that a sympathetic and munificent soul, however much subjected to cruel trials in this world of woe, always comes off triumphant over them all and gains the most adequate of all rewards—an abode in heaven.]

THE TALE.

The Consequences of Generosity.

A Bráhman woman and a milkmaid were fast friends. The latter was very poor, having hardly the wherewithal to keep body and soul together, whereas the other was immensely rich by virtue of her daily worshipping the god, Náráyana, and in reward for her great virtue. The two used to sit of an evening, and one evening the poor woman begged of her wealthy friend a favour. It was that she should lend her the image of Náráyana for a year that she too might daily worship him in her house with the view of mending her fortune. The Bráhman woman readily consented, little suspecting what might follow such a step. On the next day the image changed hands.

From this time on, as by magic, the poor milkmaid began to grow in affluence, while the reverse became the case with her generous friend. Her riches soon dwindled away to nothing; her friends, relatives, and servants fled from her, and she herself and her husband had not the means of living from day to day. They then resolved to leave their home, where poverty was unbearable, and try to live unknown in a strange land.

The first place they went to was the house of a woman of bad repute who had been once a *rayát*[1] of theirs. She, of course, did not recognise them in their changed condition, when they offered themselves to serve her for a living. They were employed by her as man and maid servants, but it was not long before they lost their situations. One day, as the Bráhman was scouring a cup it sank beneath the ground; and, as fate would have it, the Bráhman woman, while she was cooking, had her bread, curry, and all other things burnt to cinders. For these faults they were instantly dismissed from the house.

They next appealed to a former friend, who also did not recognise them, for help. He gave them half a seer of rice and an unripe plantain which they, in disgust at the miserliness of the donor and the scantiness of the dole, buried in the ground and came away.

After this they came to the house of a daughter of theirs who had been married to a rich man. She too did not know them, so dreadfully had penury changed them. The woman got a place there as a nurse. Within a few months of the appointment she was one morning given the charge of a child of her daughter's, while the latter went away to the *ghát* to

[1] A tenant.

fetch water. Now, the child began crying in an extraordinary way and would not be quieted. The woman drew the figure of a peacock on the ground wherewith to divert the mind of the little rogue and placed on its neck a chain of gold belonging to the child. And behold! the peacock rose from the ground alive, and swallowed the chain, and flew away. When the mother of the child returned home, she missed the ornament and said in great anger to the nurse,

"It is you, woman, who out of avarice have stolen the chain of gold."

And the nurse, her mother, replied, "It was the picture of a peacock that rose from the ground alive that swallowed it. I am not the thief."

At this the woman laughed scornfully and turned her and her husband out of doors.

But just at this time the year for which the Bráhman had lent her image of Náráyana to the milkwoman had lent her image of Náráyana to the milkmaid was completed, and she returned with her husband to the home they had deserted. She brought back the image from her friend's house to her own and installed it upon its throne and worshipped it rather more devoutly for having tasted of very great adversity. And with the god returned all her former wealth, her relatives, and friends, and servants; and she once more was able to practise her liberality upon the old scale.

The Bráhman woman one day bethought herself of the woman of bad repute, of her friend, and of her daughter who had all treated her so ill in her adversity. She called at their houses one by one. To the first woman she said,

"Were you not my tenant, and did you not turn me and my husband out cruelly?"

To which the woman replied, "Alack, I did not know who you were or I would have sung and danced for joy when you came to my house. I would rather have been myself turned out of my own house than have turned you out of it." She also told her that the cup which had been lost had reappeared in a strange way.

To the friend she said, "Were you not a friend, and how could you give me and my husband half a seer of rice and an unripe plantain?"

The friend said, "I did not know who you were or I would have given you all I had and lived upon half a seer of rice and an unripe plantain myself."

To her daughter she said, "Were you not my daughter, and did you not call me a thief and deny me, your mother, and your father as well who was with me the shelter of your roof?" The daughter wept tears of sorrow and said,

"Mother, why did you not tell me you were my mother and he, my father? I would not then have called you a thief and denied you and my father the shelter of my roof."

While they were thus talking, the figure of a peacock came flying through the air and deposited the lost chain of gold at the feet of the daughter.

Thenceforward the Bráhman woman and her husband lived happily in the enjoyment of the wealth which had returned to them by the favour of Náráyana and made gifts as usual, to all comers. The gods, *Pitris* (manes), and guests were always served with liberality in the house.

So, ye all that have listened to this sacred *kathá*, cry victory to Náráyana;—*ulu! ulu! ulu!*

NOTE.—The reader will mark the coincidences between this story and that of *Nala and Damayanti* in the Mahábhárat. It is evident that the older story has been condensed and slightly transformed in this *kathá* current among our womankind. In the case of Nala it was the wrath of Kali, a malignant deity, that was the cause of the untold misery the royal couple had to endure, as in the present case it was the transference of the sacred image that plunged the pious family into great distress. The swallowing of the chain of gold by the picture of a peacock has been transplanted bodily into this *kathá*. Amongst all the duties of householders, that of making gifts to Bráhmans and mendicants has been pronounced to be the highest. These people depend for their sustenance upon the householder. To this day, in Hindu India, the house is abominated from which a beggar returns without receiving his dole. The *Dán Sankránti* ceremony is very popular in Bengal, and gifts of various kinds are distributed among Bráhmans whenever it is performed.

XI.

THE KÁLIKÁ CEREMONY.

[A small earthen jar painted white and vermilion is placed upon a small altar and forms the object of worship. The goddess, of course, fills it with her spirit. The worshipper is to try to have before her mind's eye the appearance of the goddess described in the following verses which are muttered low :—

" Fierce-faced, dark, and with hair dishevelled,
Thou that hast four arms and a neck-lace of human heads round thy neck,
In thy left hands that are raised there are a conch-shell and a sword,
Thy right a quoit and a lotus adorn,
Thou that art naked but for a robe of human hands,
Bespattered with blood, three-eyed, and mounted upon the body of Siva, thy lord ! "

The goddess is celebrated in the Bhabishya Purán.]

THE TALE.

A Bráhman's Ban.

ONCE upon a time Indra, king of the gods, gave a party at Amarávati. *Apsarás* and *Kinnaris* were singing, and playing, and twirling round and round, and bouquets of flowers were flying about among them and the audience. It was a mad hour of unbridled merriment. An old Bráhman was shown in, and he blessed Indra with a Bráhman's blessing, but the unfortunate king of the gods, instead of coming down to salute his feet, returned his generosity by flinging at him a bunch of flowers he had just received from a dancing beauty. It was in mere wantonness of glee and thoughtlessly done, but the high-spirited old Bráhman determined not to take it in that light, and working himself up into a white heat of passion, cursed Indra on the spot, saying,

"Darest thou, king of the gods, insult a holy Bráhman thus, and defile his person with flowers received from the hands of a dancing girl? Thou shalt rue thy hardihood, king of the gods though thou art. By my word, thou shalt expiate thy crime by having to live the life of a cat for twelve full years in the house of a huntsman on earth!"

The Bráhman then hurried out of the hall.

The whole audience was terrified; and to the sound of music there presently succeeded the sound of wailing. The songstresses stopped in the middle of a tune, and the dancers did not finish the dance. Indra had swooned upon the throne and died as soon as the curse had been uttered. The soul of the god was transplanted into the body of a kitten and so it befell that Indra was re-born in the form of a cat.

Now Sachi, the queen of heaven, was unconscious of the transformation of her lord, as she was away from home when the calamity happened to him. Attended by her handmaid, Rati, the paragon of feminine charms, she was in her delightful park of Nandan coquetting with flowers and chasing the bees. It was some days before she came home, and when she arrived, she was greatly astonished at her husband's absence. She was at a loss to account for it, as she knew that heaven was in profound peace, and that no warfare was going on with the *Dánavas* (giants) requiring his presenee in the camp. Her anxieties deepened into fear ; and the affeetionate wife neither ate nor slept but looked as if she would wear herself to death. Then the gods came and waited on her. It was by them she was told what a terrible fate had overtaken her lord, and that it was her portion now to try to deliver him. The first thing they eounselled her to do was to seek out the Bráhman—the maker of the misehief—and to propitiate him. He might tell her where her husband had been re-born and how he might be redeemed.

So Sachi started upon her errand, and wandered through all the three worlds, and rested not till she had found the mischief-maker. The Bráhman was a hermit of great sanctity and was, by virtue of his piety, mightier than gods and men. Sachi was fortunate in finding the Bráhman in good humour and when she told him that she was Sachi, he was filled with admiration at her courage in eoming to him and knew not how to serve her sufficiently.

"Great queen of heaven," said he, "you have been pleased to sanetify my hermitage with the dust of your feet—it will redound to your glory ; I am gratified ; the fruits of my devotions have been attained."

But it was not to be flattered that Sachi had come. She sweetly begged to be exeused for having interrupted the holy man in his devotions ; and then folding her hands in the attitude of a supplicant,

"Great hermit," said she, "you know my husband, the king of the gods, is now expiating his crime of having insulted you in the shape of a cat. O, it is a cruel sentence, a very cruel one! Is there no remedy? Can there be no palliation?"

"Indráni,"[1] replied the Bráhman in a tone of compassion, "I would revoke the curse if it could be revoked. You know a pious Bráhman's word must take effect and cannot be undone even by himself. Your husband has no choice but to suffer his term of penalty. But I will do this for you—the utmost that I can do—I will tell you where he now is and how you may best help him."

He then informed the goddess where the huntsman was in whose house her lord now lived as a cat and advised her to worship the great Káliká for his benefit. "This goddess," concluded the holy man, "if pleased, will find some means of mitigating the miseries of Indra's lot."

The two then parted.

Arrived at the house of the huntsman, Sachi discovered the cat, her husband, and was quite overcome with grief. The cat too seemed to retain some knowledge of his former self, and mewed round and about her, and caressed her as if craving for sympathy. The wife of the huntsman, Subhadrá, was a very good woman and enlightened for one of her low caste. She welcomed Sachi with *pádya* and *arghya* and pressed her to eat of what she had, though Sachi had not told her, and did not mean to tell her, who she was. Casting off her state and dignity, the faithful wife had donned the garb of a common mortal and decided to abide in the house of the huntsman in order to be near her lord. She remembered the advice of the hermit and worshipped the great Káliká with a singleness of heart that highly pleased the goddess. She appeared to

[1] Wife of Indra.

Sachi in her proper person. She knew why she had been worshipped.

"Gentle Sachi," said she, "I cannot undo what the hermit has done nor can I reduce the term of the penance. I can only lessen the miseries of such an existence. If you will, I can make the cat, your lord, and yourself, sleep such a deep sleep as will last you the rest of the period; and this will save him his sufferings and you your weariness and impatience, and the whole long, long time will pass like a minute."

Sachi gladly accepted the proposal. And she slept with the cat in her embrace in the house of the huntsman through many a day that gathered into months and months that gathered into years. And when they awoke at the end of the appointed term, the cat was no more a cat, but the splendid king of the gods himself, and Sachi stood by his side beaming with joy and love. To the good huntsman and his wife they were as liberal as you could have wished them to be, and they returned to their home in heaven where great festivals were held in honour of their arrival.

The goddess Káliká who was first worshipped on earth by Sachi had her rights gradually established in this world, and is, to this day, worshipped by men of all climes and conditions.[1]

So, ye all that have listened to this sacred *kathá*, cry victory to Káliká;—*ulu! ulu! ulu!*

[1] Though this is the traditional account of the origin of Káli or Káliká worship, yet the Pauránic account is different. We read in the Puráns that Káli was a manifestation of Sakti (strength), and that she first appeared in the war of the gods with the *Dánavas* headed by Sambhu and Nisambhu. The goddess is worshipped with more devotion in Bengal than anywhere else.

XII.

THE SATYA PIR PUJÁH.

[This is one of the most popular ceremonies in the Lower Provinces in which women take part. To the deity worshipped is attached a strange tradition. The common notion is that he is no other than Vishnu himself under another name; but there is a curious touch of low Muhammadanism in the whole *Pujáh*. The cognomen, Náráyan, is considered synonymous with *Pir*—a Muhammadan appellation for a saint. It is mentioned in the "Brataratnamálá" that the Muhammadan Pir is the same as the Hindu Náráyan, and that the Vedas do not differ from the Korán. The fact is that this *Pujáh* came to be in vogue at a time when Islam had attained great proportions in India, and when everything Hindu, even religion itself, had been tinged with the faith of the conquerors. The *Pujáh* may be celebrated any time in the year excepting in the inauspicious months of January and March and on the astrologically evil days.]

THE TALE.

The Pir's Power.

A BRÁHMAN was trudging along his accustomed round of begging when a Muhammadan fakir accosted him, enquiring, "Whither bound, friend?"

On being told his mission, he said, "Why don't you worship Satya Pir and she would save you the humiliation of depending on charity?"

"Why?" replied the other, "can it be that the

Pujáh of Satya Pir is so efficacious that I would not have to beg again ? Whether it is so or not I should be false to my religion if I were to change. Do you mean that I who am a Bráhman and have worshipped Náráyan all my life can forswear my religion and bend before the false god of the *Mlechcha* (the unclean) ? "

"And pray, what has your god done for you ?" returned the fakir. "After the devotion of nearly a lifetime you are still a miserable beggar."

The Bráhman admitted that that was true, but he was confident of salvation after death.

"This much, at least," he said, "Náráyan will do for me. I cannot be unmindful of the welfare of my soul even to oblige your Pir, my friend."

"You are mistaken, brother," said the fakir, "you do not fall by worshipping the Pir whom you would call a *Mussalman god.* God does not belong to any nation or people in particular. He is among all peoples the same. Ram differs from Rahim just as little as the Vedas do from the Korán ; only the manifestations are different according to the necessities of the different ages of creation. I offer you Pir ; he is the god of the age, and your reward will be great."

"How will he reward me ?" enquired the Bráhman, partly convinced.

"The boon," replied the stranger, "is according to the prayer of the worshipper. Are you poor ? You will no longer have any poverty to bemoan. Are you childless ? and do you wish for a child ? You will have your wish. The sick will recover health ; and the seeker after fame will get it, if he prays for it."

Whereupon the Bráhman there and then resolved that he would worship Satya Pir. His new friend instructed him what were to be the offerings to the god. They consisted of one and a quarter seers of flour or pounded rice and the same measure of milk and sugar besides the indispensable present of flowers and *bel*-leaves.

That night the Bráhman performed the *Pujáh* with what he had got by begging; and his fortune changed. In a few days it was noised about the country that the Bráhman had lighted upon hidden treasure and had become immensely rich.

The Bráhman had a neighbour—a rich merchant, Dhanapati by name, who had no children to gladden his heart and that of his wife, Lilábati, and to inherit the wealth of his house. He took the advice of the Bráhman and performed a grand *Pujáh* to Satya Pir with the object of having a child. And immediate was the manifestation of the favour of the god; for Lilábati was delivered of a female child within a year. She grew up to be a charming girl and rejoiced in the name of Kalábati, which means a moon. When she attained a marriageable age, she was wedded with great pomp to Sankhapati, a young merchant of great promise.

A couple of years afterwards, the father-in-law and son-in-law fitted out a large fleet, and filled it with a rich cargo, and set sail for South Pátan—the kingdom of Raja Kalánidhi. They reached that country in good time, but had not established themselves at the capital for many days before it happened that a rich necklace of gold was stolen from the person of the princess, the king's daughter. The thief sold it to Dhanapati who, not knowing that it was stolen, shortly afterwards made a present of it to Sankhapati, his son-in-law. The officers of the king arrested Sankhapati with the ornament on his person and in spite of the protestations of the two merchants, brought them both before the king who threw them into prison and confiscated all the property that they had in their warehouses and strong boxes.

Years rolled on, but there came no change in the fortunes of the poor merchants ; and Lilábati and Kalábati's anxiety for the safety of their husbands increased. In their agony of mind they sought the help of Satya Pir and worshipped him with as much fervour of devotion as their hearts were capable of.

Satya Pir who was as easily pleased as offended smiled upon them and promised in a dream, as was his wont, to restore their husbands to them. He had been offended in that Dhanapati had not kept his promise of a magnificent *pujáh* on his obtaining a child for a boon. Was it not many years since he had got the lovely Kalábati, and had he yet fulfilled his promise ? Such thankless creatures were men. At last the Pir was propitiated and that very night the king who had condemned Dhanapati and Sankhapati had a startling vision through his agency. The sleeper perceived a glorious being standing by his bedside who commanded him, on pain of annihilation of himself and his house, to release the two merchants, Dhanapati and Sankhapati, whom he had unjustly sentenced to perpetual imprisonment. They were his followers, he said, and they were undeserving of the treatment meted out to them.

The king, of course, lost not a minute in obeying the mandate of the dread god. He, himself, struck the fetters off the feet and hands of his prisoners, and then feasted them royally in his palace, giving them the most valuable presents.

So, after many a year of captivity they emerged again and, as privileged people, made large profits out of their merchandise, which had been restored to them by order of the king. After reaping the fruits of their labours, they set out on their homeward voyage.

When about halfway home an old man called out to Dhanapati from the shore, "Hullo, merchant, what is it you have loaded your ships with?"

And Dhanapati, in the pride of his heart, answered, "With creepers and leaves of trees." And lo! the heaps of gold and other valuable things on board instantly turned into creepers and leaves of trees.

Dhanapati was overwhelmed with grief and wept like a child. His son-in-law, however, suspected that there was something more than human in the common old man asking about the merchandise, and swam ashore to where the old fellow stood laughing in his sleeve. He threw himself at his feet, and addressed him with many a humble word of penitence and grief, and invoked his mercy. The strange old man was propitiated and relented.

"Go back to your ships," said he, "and tell your father-in-law that it was Satya Pir whom he had the hardihood to taunt. Go back and rejoice, for your goods have regained their old condition."

They then sailed again rejoicing and reached home favoured by wind and tide. Their trials were now ended, and they were received into the bosom of their family after many weary years of separation. They did not forget that Satya Pir, who had caused them to be buried alive in a dungeon and had converted their gold into creepers and leaves of trees, could ruin them again if they should offend him by neglecting to render him the tribute that was his due.

So, ye all that have listened to this sacred *kathá*, cry victory to Satya Pir ;—*ulu! ulu! ulu!*

Our own idea of Satya Pir *pujáh* is that, under the persecution which the Hindus suffered at the hands of the Islamites in India, the Bráhmans and their folk carried on their own religious rites under colours slightly false, and in this way Satya-Náráyana came to be called Satya Pir. The rites of worship are not many. These, again, are not at all attractive. Simple in their character, they may be gone through within the privacy of the Hindu home. The name, therefore, was in such a case everything, the object being to delude Mussulmans into a belief that it was no Hindu deity, but a Mussulman saint who was being worshipped. No image, be it noted, is made of Satya Pir. The low class Mussulmans also worship him. They, however, set up an emblem which consists of an umbrella rolled up and a brazen stick with a circular plate at its top. Both the rolled-up umbrella and the stick are planted in the earth.

The other theory is that low class Hindus began to actually worship Mussulman pirs or local saints. This went on for some time, till the Bráhmans slightly changed the name of Satya Pir into Satya-Náráyan. This was easy, considering that no image was set up of the deity worshipped. The great Chaitanya, on the other hand, was for some time worshipped by many ignorant Mussulmans under the name of "Pir Goráchánd." Goráchánd is a name of Chaitanya. His sanctity entitled him to the rank of a *pir* in the estimation of Mussulmans.

XIII.

THE SUBACHANI CEREMONY.

[The goddess Subachani has four faces looking four ways and has a *kamandalu* (an anchorite's alms-pot) in one of her hands. Her complexion is like that of a red lotus. She is one of the incarnations of Durgá or Sakti—the wife of Siva. The *pujáh* is celebrated on Tuesdays and Saturdays in any part of the year.]

THE TALE.

The Gander-eater.

In the country of Kalinga there lived a poor Bráhman widow who had an only son. She had placed him at the village school where he had made friends with some lads, sons of well-to-do people and accustomed to dainty eating. The young people had once upon a time a chat about what they ate at home, and Satyabrata, our hero, discovered that whereas his companions regaled on fish and flesh in plenty, he had nothing but vegetables—a widow's fare. He was much pained. And sorrowful and humiliated he went home to his mother, crying and sobbing.

"Mamma," said he, "why do you feed me with vegetables while they all—my school-fellows—sit down to savoury dishes of fish and flesh?"

It was with tears trickling down her cheeks that the mother replied, " They eat, my child, as they have been provided for. Where shall I, a poor woman, get fish and flesh for you, my darling—I who can scarcely get enough to keep ourselves from starving ? "

" That won't do," retorted the spoilt child, " I must have meat to eat or I will not eat at all. If you can't get it, mamma, I'll get it myself."

And what did he do ? He was true to his word. In the evening of that same day the mother saw with horror in her son's hand a dead gander plucked and ready for cooking. She knew it was dishonestly come by, but had not the courage to remonstrate for fear of driving him into a fit of ill-humour. She cooked the meat without a word and felt a sense of relief only when it was all eaten up and apparently there was not a bone to tell the night's tale.

But a guilty deed can scarcely be concealed. In the morning when it was discovered in the royal aviary that one of the ganders was missing, parties were sent out in every direction to find out, if possible, what fate had befallen the pet. One of these men discovered the feathers and quills of the bird in a part of the Bráhman widow's house, and the truth was not long in oozing out. Satyabrata was immediately placed under arrest and taken to the king who, beside himself with indignation, sentenced him to perpetual imprisonment.

The poor mother, on receiving the news of her son's fate, ran up and down the village maddened with grief and knew no consolation. But providentially she saw some people worshipping a strange goddess with all the rites of a correct *pujáh* and she inquired about it. They told her the goddess was Subachani—the donor of all boons.

"Good woman," said they, "if you can please her, there is nothing you can wish for but shall be fulfilled." They further told her how the *pujáh* was to be performed.

She came home directly and casting aside her grief for the time addressed her whole soul to the pious work. The goddess was not hard to please, and before long she spoke in a sweet voice to the woman, as she lay prostrate on the ground before her image, saying,

"I am pleased with you; what is it you wish for?"

And the woman replied as in a trance,

"If you are pleased, mother, let my son, Satyabrata, be released from the king's prison, and let good fortune attend him now and for ever." The answer came close upon the prayer, "It shall be so."

And the woman rose from the ground, and hope returned to her careworn heart.

Just at this time the king in his palace felt very heavy and inclined to sleep, and he lay down where he was and soon was in a deep slumber. All this was the work of Máyá—the handmaid of the goddesses of heaven. Hardly had the king laid himself down before he saw a strange sight and heard a strange voice. It was the goddess Subachani who stood at his bedside, lighting up the whole room with a halo circling her divine person and filling it with soft fragrance. To him she said,

"King, I do not mean you ill; but I cannot bear to see you maltreat the son of a worshipper of mine, Satyabrata, the Bráhman lad whom you have condemned to prison to-day. He must be set at liberty at once, and what is more," added the goddess, "you shall marry Sakuntalá, your daughter, to him and make him heir to half your *ráj*. This must be done with all possible speed or woe betide you and your luckless race! As for the gander that was missing, it is even now in the aviary as much in possession of life and limb as you are yourself."

The goddess vanished in a flood of light, and the king started to his feet, wild with terror. To run to the prison, to strike off the shackles from the hands and feet of Satyabrata, and to carry him with royal honours to the palace, were for the king the work of a few minutes. The royal astrologer was consulted, and fixed an hour that very evening for the nuptials of the princess Sakuntalá and Satyabrata. They were duly solemnized and the dowry was half a kingdom.

Conceive the joy of Satyabrata's mother when instead of the hourly-expected news of the death of her erring son by impalement, she heard of his joyous progress homeward with a princess for a bride and half a kingdom for her dowry. All this was the gift of the munificent deity whom she had worshipped with so much devoutness. Mother Subachani she never forgot, neither did her posterity; and they always worshipped her with an ever-increasing zeal.

So, ye all that have listened to this sacred *kathá*, cry victory to Subachani;—*ulu! ulu! ulu!*

XIV.

THE NIL-SASHTHI CEREMONY.

[This is the only Sashthi *pujáh* performed in the dark fortnight. The season is the month of November or December. The goddess is a transformation of the wife of Vishnu according to some, of the wife of Siva according to others. The rites differ from those observed in the worship of the other Sashthis.]

THE TALE.

The Fatal Oath.

A BRÁHMAN had two sons and a daughter. The latter had been married and lived not far from her father's home. The wife of the Bráhman fell ill and died and her *Srádh* ceremony (obsequies) was performed. Now her daughter who was called Bijayá had not the least knowledge of the illness or death of her mother. Though she lived not very far from her father's home, she had not heard anything about her family for long and was naturally anxious to learn how the world went with them all.

So, upon an auspicious day, she took leave of her father-in-law and mother-in-law and called at her father's house. Her grief knew no bounds at being told of the death of her mother. The wife of her eldest brother was not at home. The other sister-in-law took her by the hand and said, "Sister, comb my hair and make yourself useful."

Bijayá was very sad and said through her tears, "Sister, if mother were living, she would have pressed me to some refreshment after the journey I have taken and not have asked me to comb her hair and make myself useful."

But she did as her sister-in-law wished, and after a while inquired of her if she knew whom her late mother had entrusted with the worship of Sashthi—her guardian goddess. The sister-in-law said,

"Yourself, of course, her own daughter, and neither me nor my elder sister who were but her daughters-in-law."

Bijayá replied it could not be. And so, there was a long dispute between the two ; and both of them swore by their husbands and children that each was in the right. And behold! their husbands and children swooned away that instant and lay dead on the ground.

Bijayá was beside herself with grief at this new stroke of misfortune. But rightly guessing it was all owing to the goddess Sashthi taking umbrage at the oaths that had been taken, she resolved to call on her in person and ascertain what to do.

So, she set out and travelled on and on till she came to a plum tree where the path divided, and she knew not by which to go. And the plum tree cried,

"Here, damsel, I can tell you the right path, if you promise that when you have seen the goddess Sashthi, you will present her with a few of my fruits."

She promised compliance and was placed upon the right path. And Bijayá again trudged on and on till she reached the junction of two other paths. And there was a milch cow at the junction; and the cow, addressing Bijayá, said,

"Daughter, I will tell you which way to go if you will consent to carry a jugful of my milk and offer it to Sashthi, when you come to her august presence."

Of course, Bijayá took some of her milk and in return was told which path to follow. So, once again she put her best foot foremost and having travelled many and many another weary mile, she reached the banks of a river. Seeing a boat gliding along she stopped and heard the people on board talking of the *Kali-Yuga* (the modern age of sin) and singing the *Kali-Yuga*. So she concluded it could not be the boat of Sashthi and let it pass by. Then another came within hail; and in it the people were talking of piety and singing sacred songs. She, therefore, knew it must be the boat graced by the presence of Sashthi herself. Falling prostrate on the sand and calling on the goddess in a loud voice, she prayed to be taken on board and in the end her request was granted.

She was received very kindly by the goddess, to whom she related her story. She bathed her feet with tears and folding her hands in humility,

"Mother," said she, "am I to continue your *pujáh* now that my mother is dead? I shall be very happy to do it; but, mother, what of my husband and children and my brother and his children who have died in consequence of our swearing by them?"

Then the goddess said, "Get yourself to your father's home, my daughter. There upon a tamarind tree near by you will find my image deposited by a crow amongst the foliage. Take it down, and purify it with Ganges water, and worship me through it. Touch the corpses of your husband and children and those of your brother and his children—all of whom have died from your swearing by them—with the flowers offered in my *pujáh* and they shall regain life."

So saying, she vanished with the boat, and Bijayá found herself lying upon the bank.

It took her far less time to reach her father's home than it had taken her in her journey thence. On her arrival she lost not a minute in fetching the image of the goddess from the tamarind tree and in purifying it. And when the next sixth day of the moon came round, she worshipped it with due rites and ceremonies. The goddess was mightily pleased; and as soon as Bijayá had, according to her instructions, touched the corpses of her husband and children and those of her brother and his children with the flowers offered in the *pujáh*, they sprang back to vigorous life as if refreshed by sleep. And there was joy in every heart and great was the glorification of the mighty goddess Sashthi who thenceforth came to be worshipped everywhere in the three worlds of heaven, earth, and the nether region.

So, ye all that have listened to this sacred *kathá*, cry victory to mother Sashthi ;—*ulu ! ulu ! ulu !*

XV

THE MANTHAN SASHTHI CEREMONY.

[The Manthan Sashthi ceremony is celebrated in the month of September on the sixth day after the new-moon. Some pigmy figures roughly resembling the human form are made of pounded rice painted with a mixture of turmeric-water and vermilion. The goddess is worshipped with the customary offerings of flowers, *bel*-leaves, sandalwood paste, incense, rice, and blades of grass.]

THE TALE.

Sacrificed to Varuna

A BRÁHMAN from pious motives wanted to dig a pond. But however deep down he dug, water was not to be found. Whereupon the Bráhman fretted himself to sleep and dreamt a fearful dream in which he was told that unless he sacrificed his only grandson, who was an infant, to the water-god, Varuna, and cut his body into five pieces, burying them at the four corners and the centre of the excavation, not a drop of water would appear, however deep he might cut the earth. The poor Bráhman woke up with a shudder, and pondering on the dreadful vision, grew sadder and sadder at heart. Quite at a loss what to do, he did not at first tell his son anything, though the latter was very anxious to learn what the matter was with his father. But when at last the son was let into the secret, it cast a gloom over his face. Yet his affection for his father and his devotion to the god Varuna were strong enough to determine him to sacrifice his only son to save the one from the sin of an unaccomplished vow and to propitiate the other. So, after nightfall, he took his son in his arms to where the pond was being made and cut him with his own hands into five pieces and deposited the parts at its four corners and in the centre as directed. Forthwith water rushed up from every point of the pond and quickly filled it to the brim.

Now, when a pond is dug in furtherance of a vow, it has to be consecrated by rites prescribed in the *Shástras*. The ceremony was fixed for the next day. The old Bráhman invited his caste comrades to come and witness the consecration rites; and they came with the rising sun in expectation of a grand feast. He was fully aware of what his son had done and grief sat heavy in his heart. His daughter-in-law, however, did not suspect anything; and when desired to do the cooking for the guests, she gaily promised compliance. She was to wear a new pair of conch-shell bangles that day, and when she went to bathe in the new pond of her father-in-law's, she put vermilion paint on her forehead and at the parting of her hair above and took a quantity of rice-powder with which to polish her bangles. At the *ghát* it struck her as unusual that her child had not come to her the whole morning, but the attending maid-servant stopped her anxious inquiries by saying,

"Oh, has he not an aunt and a grandma to take care of him?—he is with the one or the other at home."

She then saw vessels made of the leaf-stalk of the plantain tree, with sacred hay and other offerings of *pujáh* in them floating on the water. These reminded her that it was the Manthan Sashthi *pujáh* day. She had always been a devout worshipper of Sashthi, but, strangely enough, had forgotten her that day. She now lost not a minute more, but hastily bathing, got a few of the leaf-stalk vessels together in which she arranged offerings of flowers and *bel*-leaves that were at hand. She then made an image of the goddess Sashthî with the powdered rice she had brought with her and worshipped the goddess with all the devotion of an earnest heart. And when she had done, she looked behind her and saw a very old woman with her infant in her arms standing behind her.

"You are not very careful of your child, it seems," said the woman, "or you had before this known where he has been all the morning."

She then handed over the child to the mother and vanished into thin air, for she was none other than the goddess Sashthi herself!

Awestruck and filled with the deepest feelings of love and gratitude to her guardian deity, the lady returned home, her child in her arms. And it was a sight to see how the old father-in-law and the husband stood rooted to the ground struck with amazement and joy. The old man threw himself at the feet of his daughter-in-law and cried out,

"You must be more than human; tell me who you are!"

The lady fled into her room in confusion, and when everything was narrated as to how, unknown to her, her child had been sacrificed to Varuna the night before, she told them how she had regained it by favour of the goddess Sashthi.

Then there was rejoicing all over the house, and the pious old father-in-law made an image of Sashthi in gold and placed it in his house to be worshipped by his family to the remotest descendants.

So, ye all that have listened to this sacred *kathá*, cry victory to mother Sashthi ;—*ulu! ulu! ulu!*

XVI.

THE JOYMANGALBÁR CEREMONY.

[This ceremony is performed on Tuesdays during the bright fortnight in the month of June. Images are rarely made, but a few leaves of the jack-fruit tree are dotted with vermilion and are arranged in a certain order upon a daïs. These are considered to be seats very acceptable to the goddess, who is a transformation of the wife of Shiva. Blades of grass, fruits, flowers, sandal-wood paste and *áman* paddy are amongst the offerings. The family priest conducts the *puján.*]

THE TALE.

Joyabati—the Gift of Joyá.

"It is a shame, Joyá, that I have no *puján* on earth," said the goddess Chandi walking between her maids-of-honour, Joyá and Bijoyá. Joyá replied meekly that if her mistress permitted her, she could, she trusted, have her *puján* established in the lower world in no time. The permission was gladly given, and the adventurous maiden set out for the earth, full of her great mission and enriched with the blessings of her well-wishers.

One day, at about noon, an old Bráhman stood at the gate of Kanak Sen's mansion, begging for food. Kanak Sen was a very rich merchant and father of six stalwart sons, but he had no daughter. The servant who came with food for the Bráhman was asked, "Has your master got a daughter?" The man replied in the negative. "I will have nothing from a daughterless donor," rejoined the Bráhman and turned away.

Kanak Sen was deeply hurt to learn what the Bráhman had said and immediately came to where he sat under a tree.

"Reverend sir," said he, "it gives me very great pain to think that a hungry Bráhman should turn away unfed from my door. If you will not receive entertainment at my hands because I am daughterless, why don't you kindly provide me with the means of having one?"

"This I can," replied the Bráhman, who was none other than Joyá in disguise. "Take this drug, and let your wife eat it in a spirit of meekness and faith after she has had her day's bath and with her hair dishevelled. Then in time a daughter will be born to you. Mind that you name her Joyabati; and when she is grown up to marriageable age, let her have a husband whose name is Joydev, and who is the only son of a father who has six daughters."

So saying, the *pseudo*-Bráhman vanished out of sight.

As he had said, so it came to pass. The wife of Kanak Sen took the drug, and in due time a lovely girl was born, whom, as promise-bound, he called Joyabati. The girl seemed to have been born with a turn for religion and with a pious mission to accomplish; for she sported not in her girlhood but with images of gods and goddesses and played not but at worshipping them with flowers. When she came of age, Kanak Sen sent agents in all directions to seek out the predestined bridegroom whose name was Joydev, and who was the only son among the seven children of his father. The agents had not far to go, for at a few miles from home they met with the agents of a wealthy merchant who had sent them out to seek for the girl whose name was Joyabati, and who was the only sister of six brothers, to be the bride of his son, Joydev. The agents congratulated one another, and the match was quickly concluded. The nuptials of Joyabati and Joydev were celebrated with great pomp.

In the night of the marriage, after everyone had retired to bed, Joyabati remembered she had not performed the *pujáh* of her tutelary goddess, Chandi, during the day. She got up hastily and with the few grains of paddy she found in the *baran-dálá* and a drop of vermilion from her forehead she worshipped the goddess, supplying the want of better offerings with the earnest faith of a guileless heart. Her husband. Joydev, was watching her, and when she had finished,

"Wife," said he, "what were you about all this while ?"

"Worshipping my guardian goddess, Chandi," replied she, "which I do every day."

Joydev—"What do you gain by worshipping this outlandish goddess ?"

Joyabati—"Scoff not, my lord; goddess Chandi is mighty in doing good as well as evil. As to the good that is derived from faithfully serving her, I may say briefly that by her favour lost treasures may be recovered, those who have met their death by fire or by water may regain life, and those that die in any other way may be quick again."

Joydev did not answer, but resolved to put the vaunted might of the goddess to a test. A few days afterwards, while he and his young wife were returning in a richly gilded pinnace to his own home in the south, he said to her,

"Joyabati, this part of the country is notorious as being the haunt of thieves and robbers; it is not safe, therefore, that you should keep your jewels upon your person; let me have them all in my custody."

She accordingly took them off and made them over to him. He then put them into a box and secretly threw it into the water to see if his wife could recover the treasure by favour of her goddess.

At home Joyabati was received with great tenderness by her mother-in-law and father-in-law and her husband's sisters. But they all wondered how her father could have been so niggardly as to have given her away with not even a ring of gold upon her little finger. Joyabati's maid-servant told them the truth, saying that a vast treasure in jewellery belonging to her mistress was with her husband, Joydev. In the meantime the throne of Chandi in heaven shook ominously; and she knew that some ill had befallen her worshipper, Joyabati; she also knew of what particular nature it was. So she summoned Joyá and took counsel with her. Joyá instantly let herself down to the earth and standing on the shore of the sea, summoned Rohitak, the king of the fishes, to her presence.

"Rohitak," said she, as the great fish raised itself in the water before her, "a box of jewellery has been dropped into the Krishná by Joydev; you will, at my desire, pick it up and swallow it; and also let all the fishes desert the rivers and reside in the sea, so that when Joydev's father has the river searched, he may not find any. Get yourself netted when his fishermen ransack the sea. You will be killed and cut open; but never mind that, child, for death is sweet in the service of the goddess Chandi."

Rohitak promised compliance and departed.

Now, when the new wife, Joyabati, was brought home, the relatives and friends of Joydev's family demanded a feast in commemoration of the event. A large feast required a large quantity of fish amongst other things. And Joydev's father called together hundreds of fishermen for the capture of the finny tribe. But the rivers had been abandoned by the fish as commanded by Rohitak, and not even a *punti* [1] was found. So, Joydev's father ordered a prodigiously large drag to be made wherewith to search the waters of the sea. It was made and let into the water; and when the fishermen hauled it up, what should they discover in its folds but Rohitak himself, whom, of course, they did not know. The fish was carried home in triumph, and scores of servants ran with bill-hooks to cut it to convenient pieces. But its scaly hide seemed iron-proof and not even the united efforts of a multitude could make a scratch on it. In the meantime Joyabati had an inspiration. She sent word, accordingly, through her maid to her father-in-law that if he permitted her, she would cut the fish into small pieces and make it ready for cooking. The old man laughed inwardly at the presumptuous child-wife, but determined to humour her. The spot where the fish lay was enclosed with a *purdá* (a screen) and Joyabati, a small knife in hand, took her stand inside. She had not even to lift her little finger. Invisible hands cut the fish open and took out the box of jewels it had

[1] A small fish.

swallowed by order of Joyá, and decked Joyabati's person with them. They also cut the enormous fish into small bits of meat in a very short time. When Joyabati came out of the enclosure, what was the astonishment of all and, particularly, of Joydev who saw on the person of his wife her lost jewels, to see that a mere girl had performed a feat which had baffled the strength of a multitude of strong men ! The whole of Joydev's family were so struck with admiration, that they were ready to consider her more than human, and vowed that they would not eat unless Joyabati cooked for them—Joyabati, a child of twelve. For a girl of twelve to cook for twenty times twelve people seemed impossible. But Joyabati under inspiration said that she would cook, but that she would do so behind closed doors. So, she was let into the kitchen, and the doors were shut, and there were none else within. She had only to sit down there and kill the time as best she could ; for full soon invisible hands kindled a fire ; and the cooking of the fish, and meat, and rice, and all the other things was done in a miraculously short period. Behold ! the dishes were all ready—smoking, and Joyabati's father-in-law and mother-in-law, and the relations in the house were so filled with wonder that they almost adored her.

Then, in course of time, Joyabati was delivered of a son. It was a merry day of festivity—the day on which the second *játakarma* ceremony [1] of the child was to be performed. The unbelieving Joydev, who was bent upon testing the powers of his wife's tutelary goddess, now wanted very much to see if, through her means, one who was drowned might be brought back

[1] Observance of religious rites for the well-being of the baby.

to life. And on whom, do you think, he made the experiment? Upon his own son. Before dawn, he took the infant in his arms to a deep tank and threw it into the water and stood on the bank long enough to be assured that it was drowned. He then sat up in a tree by the roadside, and when the day was far advanced, inquired of all who passed under if his family were not in mourning for the death of his child. They answered,

"Why, no! They are rejoicing at home, for it is a festal day; and just a few minutes ago, we saw your son sporting in the cradle."

The fact was that the goddess Chandi's throne had been mysteriously shaken; and apprehending some mischance to her faithful Joyabati, she had sent down Joyá to the earth, who had taken the infant under her protection when thrown into the water. And Joyabati bathing in the self-same tank had felt a something hanging by the skirts of her sadi and raising it above the surface—lo! it was her dear infant, plump, rosy, and as gleeful as ever. She was sorry to think of the hardened scepticism of her husband; for she knew it was his work and knew, too, why he had done it.

On the *Annaprashan* [1] ceremony of the child, when it was seven months old, Joydev resolved to put it to the proof if his wife's almighty goddess had enough power to save one who had been burnt to ashes. So, near the spot where in preparation for the ceremony large fires had been kindled, the wicked young man caught his playful child in his arms and suddenly threw

[1] The ceremony of giving the child rice or solid food for the first time.

him into the very centre of a furious flame. He then ran away; and climbing up a tree by the roadside, perched on a branch, and inquired of those who passed under if they knew whether his family were weeping in grief over the death of his child. They replied they knew nothing of the kind; on the contrary, they at home were in the best of spirits as it was a day of festivity, and the whole house was ringing merrily with the merry laughter of his son. What had happened was this: After the premonitory shaking of the goddess Chandi's throne, Joyá had come down once again and sat incarnate yet invisibly in the fire into which Joydev threw his boy, and in this way he had been caught up with not a hair of his head singed. When Joyabati heard of the occurrence, she sighed and exclaimed, "Ah, poor husband!"

Yet one more test remained to be made; and though quite as barbarous as the preceding ones, Joydev was resolved to make it before accepting his wife's goddess. The opportunity came, some half a dozen years later, on the occasion of the *karna-bedh* (ear-boring) ceremony of his son. As the child lay asleep in a room by itself, he produced a keen-edged sword from under his clothes, and severed its head from its body at one stroke, and concealed the parts under the bed-clothes. But his act did not escape the ever-watchful ken of the goddess Chandi nor of her adroit handmaid, Joyá, who flew down instantly with a jar of *amrita* [1] from heaven and came direct into the house where the dreadful deed had been done and where Joydev still stood contemplating it. She got the head and the trunk of the child from under the bed-clothes, and joined them, and with

[1] Nectar.

a simple sprinkling of the *amrita* on the body, revived the lad. She then addressed herself to Joydev and Joyabati, who had, by this time, joined them, saying,

"Joydev, your wife, the virtuous Joyabati, bound the goddess Chandi, the mightiest of the mighty of heaven, to work four miracles—those of recovering lost treasure, of re-animating the drowned, the burnt, and the one killed in any other way—as she had made an assertion to that effect on the night of her marriage with you. The goddess is mindful of her faithful worshipper's promises. She serves them in every way and sees that their good name does not suffer. Now, learn, Joydev, by experience and lay it to your heart that your wife's goddess is the goddess of all women and men. Worship her for temporal and eternal good and preach her glory."

Then turning to Joyabati, she said tenderly, "My child, this jar of *amrita* is the goddess Chandi's gift to her faithful worshipper. Keep it as carefully as you would your life. It has this rare virtue that a drop of it, as you saw just a while ago, can bring the dead back to life. Waver not in faith."

Then she left smiling, as she went, upon Joyabati who was on her knees weeping with joy, upon Joydev who stood like a mute statue, wonder-struck, and upon the boy who was dancing merrily round the three.

Conviction was now carried home to Joydev's mind, and the hardened sceptic was now as soft and impressionable as clay. He expended a large part of his immense fortune in erecting a grand temple to Chandi and in setting up in it a gold image of the deity, and dedicated his life, and made thousands of his relations, friends, and servants do the same, to the preaching of the Chandi *pujáh*.

Joyabati's jar of *amrita* was, after her death and ascension to heaven, inherited by her sons and grandsons who divided it, a drop per head, among themselves and were the fathers of the healing art. From them are descended the physicians who now walk the earth.

So, ye all that have listened to this sacred *kathá*, cry victory to Chandi Devi ;—*ulu ! ulu ! ulu !*

XVII.

THE ARANYA SASHTHI CEREMONY.

[The Sashthis are a numerous class of female deities, various manifestations, of course, of the same goddess, the mighty dispenser of all earthly blessings. This particular Sashthi has been celebrated in the Márkandeya Purán. She is represented as a beautiful and youthful being with a smiling face and a fair complexion and bedecked with jewels and rich clothes. She has a child in her arms. The female votaresses retire to a neighbouring forest, each with a fan in her left hand and offerings carried before them. Images are not generally made. After the *pujáh*. which is performed by the family priest, the women partake of the fruits, roots, and vegetables offered. Women who have children consider it their bounden duty to observe the ceremony.]

THE TALE.

Saved from the Cat.

A MOTHER-IN-LAW and a daughter-in-law are in the scene. The children of the latter had, while yet in their swaddling clothes, been carried off one by one, nobody knew where, by the cat of the goddess Sashthi. On the last of these mournful occasions, the mother-in-law was, as a matter of course, overwhelmed with grief and resolved to call upon the goddess personally and ask what had offended her. So, she set out on her journey.

On her way she fell in, first of all, with a wood-cutter who had a heavy load of wood on his head. He addressed her, saying, "Mother Bráhmani,[1] where are you bound for ?" And on her replying, "To the abode of the goddess Sashthi," he said, "Do you, mother, just ask the goddess, when you have seen her, why this load of wood has stuck upon my head and will not be thrown off."

To this she consented and sped onward. She then came across a lime-seller who also inquired of her as to where the end of her journey lay ; and on her repeating the same reply, "Mother Bráhmani," cried he, "forget not to tell the goddess that this pitcher of lime has got unaccountably glued to my head and to learn of her how I may be relieved."

She bound herself to do him the favour and moved on her way. Her third encounter was with a cow whose breasts and teats were surcharged with milk, yet none would milk her. After the inevitable inquiry, "Mother Bráhmani, where are you going to ?" and the answer, "To the abode of the goddess Sashthi," the cow begged of her to ask the goddess why nobody milked her. "I will," said the woman, and set off again.

But before long, she was once again stopped by a mango-tree whose branches were all bending beneath the weight of the golden fruits, but which not even the fowl of the air would peck at and eat. And when it came to know the destination of the old wayfarer, it begged her services in inquiring of the goddess why it suffered. She obliged it with a promise of compliance and set off once again.

Hardly had she gone a few paces before a pond,

[1] A Bráhman woman.

brimful of pure sparkling water, lay athwart her path and would not let her on. And the pond inquired of her, "Whither bound, mother Bráhmani?" To which, "To the goddess Sashthi's"—said she. Then the pond: "I beg of you, mother Bráhmani, to do me this kindness that you learn of the goddess why my water is not drunk by any one." She would do so, she answered, and walked forward and this time reached the end of her journey without any further interruption.

She hastened into the presence of the goddess, and bowing down to the ground before her footstool, she began with her own business.

"Mother Sashthi, why does your cat carry away the babies of my daughter-in-law?"

"Because your daughter-in-law anoints herself with oil on my *pujáh*-day."

"How is she to atone for the sin—to appease your mighty wrath, mother Sashthi?" asked the suppliant.

"Listen," cried the goddess, "your daughter-in-law is shortly going to have a son, and a very rompish and unruly one he shall be. He will try to get himself oiled on my *pujáh*-days, but prevent him. When he reaches the ninth year of his age and, on an auspicious day, is going to have the lobe of his ear pierced according to the *shástras* and to wear the sacred thread, he shall snatch the razor from the barber's hand and cut off one of his ears. But let not the barber be offended and curse the child, but say soothingly,

> "*Shát, Shát*,[1] the son of my master;
> I have lost one ear, but another I have.
> So, let him live and prosper!"

---

[1] An interjection expressive of fondness.

And when he has attained the marriageable age and has gone to the house of his bride-elect on the first day of the wedding, he shall sneeze one hundred and one times in the pavilion under which the bride will wait for him. Take care that she does not take him to task for it and curse him, but say lovingly—

> "*Shát, Shát*, the son of my father-in-law
> By whose favour I shall wear
> The conch-shell bracelet and vermilion ;
> So, let him live and prosper."

"If all this be done as I say," concluded the goddess, "take my word for it, he shall no more be carried away by the cat."

The Bráhmani was delighted and in her soul she vowed to obey the goddess's directions to the very letter. Herself satisfied, she next did the missions of her acquaintances on the way. "Mother Sashthi, a wood-cutter is in a scrape, he——."

"Oh, I know it," replied the omniscient goddess, "he suffers for not having given a measure of fuel to a Bráhman who sorely needed it. Let him be more liberal now, and he shall be relieved."

"A lime-seller, mother," began the mortal again.

"He, too, is in grief for his stinginess to a Bráhman. The same atonement ; let him make a gift of his pitcher of lime to the first Bráhman he meets with."

Then perceiving that the woman had yet something more on her mind, she knew at once what it was and proceeded,

"The cow, the mango tree, and the pond are merely doing penance for causing pain to Bráhmans. The cow did not yield milk and the tree fruits to a hungry priest, and it was at the *ghát* of the pond that another thirsty Bráhman, in his eagerness to get at the water, slipped his foot and suffered. Let them make amends by a gift respectively of milk, fruits, and water to holy Bráhmans. And their troubles shall be over."

The Bráhmani bowed a parting bow and started off on her homeward journey. On the way the pond, on being told why it suffered, said,

"Where shall I get another Bráhman beside yourself? So, do take a sip of my water and save me." And she took a sip.

Farther on, the mango tree, similarly enlightened, cried, "Where is there a holier Bráhman than my benefactress? Kindly accept a few fruits." And she accepted a few.

Likewise, the cow gave her a drink of her milk, the lime-seller, his pitcher of lime, and the wood-cutter, a quantity of wood. Then she reached home.

In a short time, her daughter-in-law was delivered of a male child. He grew, and when about five years of age, on the Sashthi *pujáh* day, he could not be ruled, as was foreordained, but would anoint himself with oil. But the grandmother had been on the alert and had concealed every vessel of oil. The urchin broke away from his mother and ran to the oil-seller's and there rubbed himself with some pieces of broken jars in which oil had been kept. At that instant the dread cat of Sashthi appeared and mewed ominously, but, obedient to the least wish of his mistress, did not seize upon his intended victim.

When at nine years of age, the boy's ear-boring and sacred-thread-wearing ceremony was going to be celebrated, the barber came whose office it was to perforate the ear. The wily urchin, as predestined, snatched the razor from the unsuspecting barber's hand and, quick as thought, cut off one of his ears. But the latter took it in good part and said with warmth,

> "*Shát, Shát,* the son of my master ;
> I have lost one ear, but another I have.
> So, let him live and prosper ! "

And in truth, the boy lived and prospered.

Now it was the day of his marriage. He came to the bride's house and met her in a pavilion waiting with her maids to receive him. And as soon as he was by her side, to fulfil the prophecy, he sneezed one hundred and one times. But the girl observed good humouredly,

> "*Shát, Shát,* the son of my father-in-law
> By whose favour I shall wear
> The conch-shell bracelet and vermilion ;
> So, let him live and prosper."

Then the wedding was solemnized in due form, and the couple returned home and lived long lives of blessedness—to the joy of the doting grandmother.

So, ye all that have listened to this sacred *kathá*, cry victory to the goddess Sashthi ;—*ulu ! ulu ! ulu !*

XVIII.

THE PÁSHÁN CHATURDASI CEREMONY.

[This ceremony is performed on the fourteenth night after the new moon in the month of December. The goddess worshipped is Bana-Durgá, the wife of Siva—the god of destruction. Images are not made; but merely some blades of *kusa* (*Poa cynosuroides*, Linn.) decked out with flowers are placed round some small earthen jugs painted white and vermilion and scented with sandalwood paste. These jugs the goddess is supposed to impregnate with her presence.]

THE TALE.

The Wife who used to Eat the First Morsel.

A CERTAIN Bráhmani had a daughter-in-law, all of whose children died in the cradle. The woman was very, very unhappy and did not know how to remedy the evil. In her distress she sought the counsel of a wise man who was credited with the gift of a sixth sense and who at once divined wherein the offence lay. Accordingly, he told the woman that it was her daughter-in-law who was to blame, for she ate the first morsel of every dish that was to be offered to the gods during the ceremonies of worship. "Do you," added he, "take care that she does not have the opportunity of doing such a sacrilegious thing again."

The woman returned home resolved that her daughter

in-law should offend no more. When next time the latter was with child and the day for the Páshán Chaturdasi ceremony arrived, at cock-crow she was bidden by her mother-in-law to take a heap of clothssoiled with ink and oil to a distant *ghát* and wash them there. She was not to return home before the task was done.

When she was gone, the old woman quickly got everything ready for the ceremony—the dishes of edibles and all. The ceremony itself was gone through speedily, and when in the evening the daughter-in-law returned home exhausted and famished, she saw in the twinkling of an eye what her mother-in-law had done. Her tongue, tricked out of its first morsels, protruded itself from her mouth like an arrow of fire and entwined itself round a post in the verandah of the house. Just then the old woman stood before her with a handful of flowers and *bel*-leaves with which the goddess had been worshipped and threw them upon the tongue that had entwined itself round the post, uttering at the same time the charm—

"O tongue that shoots out so,
O tongue, it is other people's house:
O tongue, do thou contract thyself!"

And the tongue contracted itself, and resumed its normal length, and returned to its natural abode.

Since then the tongue never shot out again, and the daughter-in-law never offended by eating the forbidden first mouthfuls. The child she soon after gave birth to and all the children that were afterwards born of her never died in the cradle, but lived and were the joy of their grandmother.

So, ye all that have listened to this sacred *kathá*, cry victory to mother Bana-Durgá;—*ulu! ulu! ulu!*

'Her tongue . . . entwined itself round a post in the verandah of the house.'

Face page 139

XIX.

THE GUHA[1]-SASTHI CEREMONY.

[This *pujáh* takes place on the sixth day after the new moon in the month of December. The goddess is one of the many Sasthis celebrated in the Márkandeya Purán. She is generally worshipped more by low class people than the higher castes.]

THE TALE.

The Wife who Cooked Beef.

A Bráhman had a daughter-in-law. Having occasion to give a feast to a large number of his caste-comrades, he bade her cook some curries, amongst which there was one of tortoise flesh. When this was nearly finished the lady asked her maid to taste some of it to see if it were palatable. The maid did as she was desired and much more, so that in a short time she had eaten

[1] [Guha is another name of Kártikeya, the generalissimo of the celestial forces. He has many other names. Regarding his birth there are three different traditions. One is that he is the son of Agni (the god of fire) brought up by the presiding geniuses of the constellations called the Kirtikás. The popular belief is that he is the son of Durgá and Siva. Kártikeya or Guha is a bachelor. But some people give him a wife called Sasthi. Probably the true explanation of the name "Guha-Sasthi" is Guha and his wife Sasthi. The ceremonies as now performed have nothing to do with Guha, though his name is still retained.]

up all that was cooked. The lady was in great distress and in great fear too, as she knew her father-in-law would not forgive her the unwarrantable consumption of his favourite curry. She and her servant took counsel together, and the latter was sent away to fetch what she could procure in the way of meat. The wench hied to a neighbouring field and, coming across a tender calf, cut it in three pieces and took off a quantity of flesh from the middle. This she presented to her mistress who, without examining it to see what meat it was, placed it in the cooking pot and began to cook it.

But as it would not boil, the servant girl threshed a few onions and threw them into the pot. Suspicion now began to cloud the mind of her mistress, who feared it might be the flesh of some prohibited, unclean animal. She dared not think of it, the meat might even be beef. She determined, however, not to offer it to the assembled Bráhmans, for if her fears were realised the eating of it would destroy their caste and doom her to an eternal hell for being the responsible agent of their ruin. She told her attendant that if her foot slipped on the floor before the guests, she (the attendant) was to promptly fetch the jug of water that stood ready for use in the kitchen, and bathe her temples, and restore her to her senses.

So, when the guests had seated themselves with plantain-leaves spread out before them to eat from and were filled with expectation of the feast, the daughter-in-law, who was also to do herself the honour of distributing the food, appeared with a large dish in her hands, and, advancing, fell prone on her face upon the ground. The maid thereupon ran, as instructed, into the kitchen, seized the jug of water that stood in contact with the cooking vessels full of eatables, and hastened with it to the side of her mistress. She recovered without much ministration; but all the food that was ready to be served was rendered unclean by the touch of the servant girl who was of a lower caste. So, the Bráhmans all went away empty, but their caste was preserved, and the great object of the young woman was fulfilled. She now threw away the eatables with the pots that held them and washed the kitchen in specially-prepared water to purify it.

It was now that the servant-girl told her mistress what she had done, and that it was the flesh of a calf that she had brought. This revelation nearly drove the lady mad with the consciousness of a great sin committed and the fear of damnation. In an agony of grief she sought divine counsel; and hastily washing herself and with the indispensable gifts of flowers, fruits, *bel*-leaves, sandalwood paste, incense, and a lamp fed with *ghee* worshipped her tutelary goddess, Sasthi. The *pujáh* done, the goddess was propitiated, and told her worshipper in a voice heard only by her that she might atone for her sin by re-animating the slaughtered calf, and this could be easily done by throwing upon the carcass some of the flowers and *bel*-leaves and sprinkling over it some of the water with which the goddess had been worshipped.

This was no sooner said than the lady ran to the field and, following the directions of the goddess, brought the calf back to life. The act freed her from the sin of cow-killing, and her heart was filled with joy.

So, ye all that have listened to this sacred *kathá*, cry victory to mother Sasthi;—*ulu! ulu! ulu!*

XX.

THE CAWRÁ CAWRY CEREMONY.

[There does not appear to be any mention of this interesting ceremony in the religious literature of India. Yet it is no less popular among the women of India than any of those treated of before. It can be performed on Sundays and Thursdays only during the bright fortnight in the months of October, December, February, and April. A few *cowries* or shells form a part of the offerings; hence, perhaps, the name. The goddess is Lakshmi, the wife of Vishnu of the Hindu triad, who is invoked on a plate of copper placed upon a brass tripod. No image is made of her.]

THE TALE.

The Banished Girls.

A Bráhman widower had two daughters. The girls kept the house and cooked for their father and themselves. They had been from their earliest years devout worshippers of Lakshmi and never failed to perform the *puját* with whatever articles of offering were available. A few ears of corn gathered from the fields, two *cowries*, and a few flowers and *bel*-leaves were all that were offered by them. The goddess, however, was satisfied, for she recognised sincerity of heart, which she prized far above all that the richest could give.

One day, on the completion of the *puját*, they begged of the goddess: "Mother, grant us that our father may marry again and beget a son to perpetuate his name." The boon was given; and it so happened that that very day the father met a beautiful girl, fell in love with her, sought her in marriage, and was accepted.

The bride was fair to see, but had a dark, spiteful mind. When she had given birth to a son and when that son was grown up, she could not bear the sight of her step-daughters—Amuná and Jamuná. And when on a Sunday or a Thursday they worshipped their tutelary goddess, Lakshmi, she looked upon the whole operation with an evil eye; and would say that they were dreadful witches who would one day destroy her son, herself, and her husband. She always kept dinning this into the ears of her old, doting husband, and gave him no rest until he had consented to banish the obnoxious girls under the pretence of taking them to their aunt's.

And one dark and stormy day, a few hours before nightfall, the old Bráhman took his daughters into the midst of a large wood and left them there while they were peacefully sleeping side by side. When they woke up, they found their father gone and cried in agony:

"Lo! our father has banished us at the instigation of that vile woman—our step-mother!"

But just then, looking round, they saw a very kind-looking old woman approaching them, who, coming up, said sweetly, "You need not be cast down, poor forlorn maidens, for I am here to help you."

The woman had an air of divinity, and the girls felt such an assurance in their hearts, that they cast off all fear. The woman was none other than Lakshmi herself. Days and months passed away in the forest, and one afternoon there was a great din all around their little cottage. Shortly afterwards two or three men appeared and begged to have a drink for their masters, who were the son of the king of the country and the son of the chief minister. They had come to hunt in the woods, they said. The two girls gave them water, which they carried to their masters, who, when they had drunk, said,

"Whence have you got this sweet water? Who gave it to you?"

They in reply said: "Two beautiful maidens who live in a cottage near by and have a comely old woman to protect them."

Then the prince and the son of the minister resolved to pay the girls a visit, and said to their servants:

"Here, lead us on, for we must see these beautiful girls who live in a cottage near by and have an old woman to protect them."

And they led them on to where they had seen the two damsels under the guardianship of the old woman. The prince and his companion fell in love with the girls at the first blush. The only difficulty was that each of them very much wished to marry both. The amorous contest was, however, settled by the old woman, who decided that the prince, as the younger of the two guests, should have Jamuná—the younger of the two sisters—and that the son of the minister should be blessed with the hand of Amuná. The nuptials were then and there celebrated in proper form, the old woman giving away the brides.

Thus were the daughters of a poor Bráhman, who had been banished into the forest to perish, raised, one to be a queen, and the other to be the wife of a minister's son—all through their piety—by favour of Lakshmi. But the gods are as ready to smile as to frown; and those who in their good fortune forget their former adversity often come to grief. And such was the case with Amuná. The two girls lived blissfully for some time, loved by their husbands and in the enjoyment of all that love or money could give. Jamuná, the princess, did not for a moment forget that she owed her exalted position to the favour of Lakshmi and worshipped her as regularly as the appointed days came round, not only with richer offerings, but also with sincerer devotion begotten of grateful love. She had a beautiful child for a son, as also had her sister, Amuná. But Amuná had forgotten her goddess, and not only did she not worship her, but, sudden prosperity having turned her head, she would also resent any one's saying that she owed her position to anything but her own graces.

So, she was cursed in high heaven. Suddenly, her husband conceived a dislike to her, which in a few days deepened into hatred, and she was turned out of his home with the baby at her breast. When her sister, Jamuná, heard of all this, she sent to fetch her to her own house and there tried to soothe her grief by such attentions as a sister and royal hostess could pay. But she did not suspect until the day for the worship of Lakshmi came round that she had forgotten her goddess and that she owed her misfortunes to the offence she had given her. Even when she reminded her of this fact, she did not seem to be awakened to a sense of the enormity of her sin,—such is the blindness of a misguided mind! Jamuná, however, begged her sister to keep fasting till the middle of the day when the *puját* was to be performed. But the curse being still upon her, she ate a mouthful at an early hour in company with the children and thus broke her fast. And when her sister invited her at midday to come and do the *pujáh* with her, she said, "Sister, I have broken my fast, and cannot."

On the following *pujáh*-day, too, she had sipped a spoonful of milk with the children and had thus rendered herself unfit to take part in the worship. An evil genius still haunted her steps. Meanwhile, the earnest prayers of Jamuná had softened the heart of Lakshmi. and she removed the film from Amuná's eyes. She now perceived how black her ungrateful heart was, and how greatly she had sinned against her goddess. The penitent soul did not need a word more of admonition from her sister, but kept fasting strictly on the next *pujáh*-day, and when the ceremony was performed, she took part in it with the greatest devoutness.

And Lakshmi was merciful to her again. Great, very great must be the glory of Lakshmi and her power immeasurable, that could so change the mind of the minister's son as to make him recall his banished wife and son that very day. He repented of his inhumanity and covered his wife and son with tears and kisses. But Amuná said,

"Do not afflict yourself, my lord and husband; it is not you but myself that am to blame. You could not save me from my misfortunes. I had most wickedly offended Lakshmi and suffered in consequence of my own sin."

Then they lived harmoniously together through many a long year of bliss. And as long as Amuná lived, she never for one day neglected to worship Lakshmi, to whom she was indebted for all that she was and all that she had; and just before she was translated to heaven, she bequeathed the pious legacy of the *pujáh* to her daughters.

So, ye all that have listened to this sacred *katha*, cry victory to Lakshmi;—*ulu! ulu! ulu!*